Dancing with Cancer

MALADIES AND MIRACLES
IN STEM CELL TRANSPLANTLAND

David & Karin,
Here's to finding
hope in our story.
Wishing you the best.

Bonnie

Dancing with Cancer

MALADIES AND MIRACLES
IN STEM CELL TRANSPLANTLAND

Barry S. & Bonnie Willdorf

ISBN: 978-1541361065

Manufactured in the United States of America.

Book design by Dennis Gallagher, Visual Strategies, San Francisco.

10 9 8 7 6 5 4 3 2 1

DEDICATION

*To my children, Megan, Nina, and Julia, and sons-in-law, Michael
and Nick, who were there every step of the way with love and
support. To my grandchildren, Miriam, Silas, Noa, and Lorenzo, so
they can remember their grandfather's strength and humor. To the
many family members and friends who were the original readers
of these blog posts and emails and who laughed and cried with us,
who cooked for us, and who shared our life in all its beauty and
sadness. To Barry's angel donor, Jennifer, who gave a two-time gift
of life to our family. And finally to the amazing medical staff at
Stanford who became our friends as well as our doctors and nurses.*

In memory of those close to us who died before, during and after:

Ann Weissman	*Jean Gilbert*
Anne Murray Ladd	*John Ferrara*
Bill Parmer	*Kevin Weston*
Ed Pembridge	*Louise Milder*
Gail Packer	*Louise Travanti*
Gus Reichbach	*Sandy Campins*
Hope Reichbach	*Sandy Klein*
Jack McCloskey	*Steve Simon*
Jane Kinzler	*Susan Offner*

LIST OF ABBREVIATIONS

ATG	Anti-thymocyte globulin
BMB	Bone marrow biopsy
BMT	Blood and marrow transplant program at Stanford
CLL	Chronic lymphocytic leukemia
CMV	Cytomegalovirus
CVP	Cyclophosphamide, vincristine, prednisolone
GVHD	Graft versus host disease
ITA	Infusion treatment area at Stanford
ITP	Idiopathic thrombocytopenic purpura
NG tube	Nasogastric tube
NP	Nurse practitioner
PA	Physician assistant
PICC line	Peripherally inserted central catheter
T-PLL	T-cell prolymphocytic leukemia
TBI	Total body irradiation
TLI	Total lymphoid irradiation
WBC	White blood count

Contents

3 Preface

5 Introduction

15 Chapter One. Asymptomatic

27 Chapter Two. What's Happening?

33 Chapter Three. Changing Doctors in Mid-Stream

45 Chapter Four. The Hero's Cure

57 Chapter Five. Jumping Hurdles to a Transplant

69 Chapter Six. The Transplant—I Could've Had a V8

89 Chapter Seven. One Hundred Days

115 Chapter Eight. The Eye of the Hurricane

135 Chapter Nine. Second Bite at the Apple

161 Chapter Ten. Another Rollercoaster Ride

173 Chapter Eleven. Whack-a-Mole

191 Barry's Epilogue

193 Bonnie's Epilogue

195 Afterword

197 Appendix

203 Acknowledgments

205 About the Authors

April 2010   *Photo by Roslyn Banish*

Preface

Barry died on February 1, 2014 after a two-week hospitalization during which his cancer relapsed. He had written the final edits to this manuscript two days before he entered the hospital. He died peacefully at home surrounded by his family.

June 29, 1968

Introduction

As I write this, it has been more than eight years since I was first diagnosed with CLL, chronic lymphocytic leukemia. I have had two stem cell transplants and been hospitalized about two dozen times. On one occasion, a rare form of leukemia, T-PLL, migrated into my stomach resulting in a miserable month in the hospital. Yet, the fact is that, thanks to exceptional medical care, good luck, and not the least, my loving wife Bonnie, I am still around and enjoying life as much as this disease will allow. This book is about all of those things that kept me alive.

When I was first diagnosed with leukemia, I felt an ominous foreboding. I'd had a brush with prostate cancer four years earlier and confided to Bonnie, during some emotionally charged pillow talk, that I was confident I'd beat the prostate cancer; but this leukemia was going to get me. I was depressed and angry. Bonnie was in denial. But when I caught my breath, I realized that what I had was all I had, and I could either make the most of it or throw away the rest of my life.

I am not a conventionally religious person. I was not raised with any religious exposure, except in school and, curiously, in the Cub Scouts. Our leader, a rabbi, spent most of his time teaching us Bible stories rather than how to tie knots. Public elementary school in the 1950s began each day with a pledge of allegiance and a Bible reading. When we got old enough to read, our teachers handed us the Bible in turns and told us we could select the passage of our choice. The Bible was a big mystery to me—a great scary unknown that had never crossed my parents' threshold. But I soon came to find an affinity for the Twenty-third Psalm—particularly the part about the valley of the shadow of death and fearing no evil. Growing up in the 1950s, there was a lot of fear and evil that trickled down from elders quaking over communism, McCarthyism, and atomic bombs, and here was an ancient passage, regardless of the God part, that told us not to fear. Its inherent contrarianism instinctively resonated with me. Then I learned that the president at the time I was born, Franklin D. Roosevelt, had said much the same thing as we entered World War II. In middle age, I was introduced to a quote from the eighteenth century rabbi, Nachman of Breslov: "All the world is a very narrow bridge, but the main thing is to have no fear at all." Would I fear my cancer, I wondered, contemplating the words of this rabbi; or would I internalize the wisdom of the ages and sages? Only time would tell.

* * *

My knee-jerk reaction to my leukemia diagnosis was to want to keep it under wraps, something relatively unusual among my contemporaries. These days, cancer patients write books such as this one because they are eager to share their experiences and get the word out.

When I was diagnosed with prostate cancer a few years earlier, I wanted to know about other men's experiences with the disease. Without much difficulty I was able to find a book right on point: *Hit Below the Belt: Facing Up to Prostate Cancer* by Dr. F. Ralph Berberich, who spoke very candidly about his own experiences, including sexual. I then went to a reading where he responded openly to every question. But I was not ready for self-revelations just yet.

When I was diagnosed with leukemia, I was asymptomatic. To my way of thinking, I could pass for being cancer-free. How many of us, I wondered, are walking around asymptomatic, thinking we're healthy? Isn't it better to pass than to bear the stigma, receive the sympathy and face the unspoken fears of others that what you have might be catchy? Why go into it? Why choose to identify yourself as sick, when you still look and feel healthy? Identifying as a cancer patient required a whole self-image makeover and I didn't want any part of it.

Perhaps I was reverting to the experiences of my youth when discussions of cancer were not so open and honest. When I was a teen, it was common for doctors to withhold a diagnosis of cancer from their patients. The diagnosis was something to be whispered first to a family member, in confidence.

Not long after I first got my driver's license, it fell to me to chauffer my grandfather to medical appointments. He had been in and out of Beth Israel Hospital in Boston over the preceding several years getting portions of his guts snipped off and being sewn back together, but during all that time no one told him what it was all about. By 1962 his intestines were like an old suit that had been altered to the point where there were no more places that could be nipped or tucked. At one of those appointments, I happened to overhear the dreaded "C" word.

When I got home I asked my mother and uncle about this cancer. They were hesitant and wanted to know how I'd heard about it. Only after I told them about my overhearing a doctor or nurse did they reluctantly admit that, yes, Zayde had cancer. Then they swore me to silence, as if it was they who'd imparted this big secret upon condition I wouldn't tell him what I'd found out from others. I recall a sense of amazement that they had concealed this news from their father for upwards of six years. I was disappointed that they had chosen lying over honesty, that they had assumed this role with arrogance, and had attempted to enlist me into their deceptive conspiracy.

Then came the inevitable next hospitalization. I found myself alone with Zayde at his bedside as he recuperated from yet another of the surgeries. He was propped on pillows looking pale and haggard and said that he wasn't sure he wanted to have any more cutting. He couldn't understand why they had to keep doing it. Why, he asked, couldn't they just get it right?

I had the choice of shrugging and being complicit in my elders' lies or I could tell the truth. "Zayde," I said, "Hasn't anyone told you that you have cancer?"

A half-smile briefly flitted across his face as he recalled something, probably a recently planted lie by one of his children, and then, just as suddenly it disappeared, replaced by a grimace. "Kensuh, huh? I thought so." We said no more about it.

A while later, my uncle Lou confronted me in the hospital corridor with my mother standing right behind him biting her lip. Lou was a big, powerful man who'd been a master sergeant in the Army, and when he loomed, when he yelled, he could be scary and intimidating. "Did you tell Harry that he had cancer?" he growled, his face red with anger.

"Yeah," I replied. "How come you've been lying to him?"

Lou was taken aback. My mother piped up, as she often did when she felt the advantage slipping. "You weren't supposed to tell."

"He asked," I said. "You want to make a liar out of me too?"

I remember that these simple comments ended our conversation. What were they going to say? "Yes, you should lie."

My family's concerns, whatever they may have been, proved to be unfounded. Zayde was able to take the news. While no one likes to hear that they are going to die, a lot of us get that information before we do die and I am convinced that most of us can take it. I believe that learning that death is rapidly approaching, as opposed to being an eventuality, can be liberating. Many of us want the time to prepare—to say our goodbyes, to complete unfinished business. And a big part of that is being forthcoming, open, and honest, rather than wasting energy on lies, half-truths, and concealments.

These days, such a disclosure—from doctor to family member while bypassing the patient—might even be considered unlawful as a breach of HIPAA (the government's patient confidentiality rules). Perhaps having better odds of survival has something to do with the increase in candid discussions of disease. Perhaps it's just another example of the "tell all" nation we have become. Nowadays there is plenty of information out there. Some of it is worthless and some of it just plain scary, but some of it is useful and inspirational. I think we are the better for all of it because at least we are talking.

Today Bonnie and I get calls—on average one a month—from people who want to know about our experience. They are often looking for encouragement because our story gives them hope. We tell them we believe that each of us must find his or her own path. We explain that they are unique and so is their cancer. We assure them there are as many different cancers as there are people who have been diagnosed with it. If that means anything, it means that, while the statistics may be helpful predictors of outcome in the general sense, they cannot possibly translate into firm odds for any particular person. Our experience attests to that, and in that sense, it has offered hope to some with a dire prognosis.

* * *

BONNIE:

Very few of us, when entering a relationship, expect to become a caregiver. Even fewer are ready to shoulder that burden at a moment's notice.

The prospect of having to care for a loved one is daunting, no matter how skilled or competent in health care matters you may be, and on top of all the emotions her or his illness evokes, you have a bunch of new responsibilities and the guilt that could follow if you screw it up.

When Barry was diagnosed with leukemia, I was immediately daunted. I'm squeamish and can't even look at a cut, much less treat it. During all of the years of childrearing, it was Barry who took out the splinters and bandaged the wounds that are an inevitable part of childhood.

It helped that Barry and I were in a long-term marriage. We knew each other very well and weathered many crises. We first met on the plaza in front of the main administration building, Low Library, at Columbia University in October 1967, the day Che Guevara was killed in Bolivia. Those were times of political ferment and many student groups had set up tables in the center of campus to attract students with literature about their organizations.

We met at the SDS (Students for a Democratic Society) table. I was a sophomore at Barnard and Barry was in his second year at the Law School. The talk, of course, was about how our revolutionary hero, Che, had just been reported killed. Three of us spontaneously decided to lower the flag to half-mast. We scampered up the wide granite steps of Low Library and began lowering the Stars and Stripes. We were almost done when a campus cop confronted us. After a little pushing and shoving the flag was hoisted back up. We started dating a few weeks later and, against the common trend of just living together, decided to get married.

April 1968. Barry third from right on Low Library Ledge, Columbia University

In April 1968 we were part of the occupation of campus buildings that SDS led. We were arrested together, along with over seven hundred other students. When my parents came to the jail, my mother's first question was, "Is the wedding still on?" I thought it was ridiculous, but now, after having produced three weddings, I get her question.

After I graduated in 1970, Barry got a $5000 grant from a civil liberties organization to provide civilian legal support to anti-Vietnam War and minority active-duty GIs. We traveled to Oceanside, California to join a small group of civilians and ex-military who were organizing Marines at Camp Pendleton. The house we moved into, a dilapidated stucco bungalow sitting among patches of brown weeds, had just been machine-gunned a few weeks earlier, and a Marine was wounded. We arrived to find it protected by sandbags and some barbed wire. That night we learned that, among the duties of this collective, was to become armed guards after sunset. We were heading for a war zone and the risks we were taking brought us closer.

After the grant expired, Barry was kicked out of the collective for his "bourgeois tendencies" (he was a lawyer after all) and I was given the choice of staying with him or with the collective. The night I had to make this choice, we hitchhiked to San Francisco and the collective dissolved a couple of months later.

For awhile I worked in the GI Movement, primarily finding lawyers for GIs who were being court martialed or wanted to apply for conscientious objector status. We were basically living from hand to mouth as Barry was still defending impoverished GIs. Then our landlord, who was having IRS troubles, offered to sell us the house we were renting. We traded our van and a thousand dollars for the house and became homeowners. The mortgage was less than our rent.

On Christmas day, 1973, we had our first child, Megan. By then I was working as a secretary, and felt that without a graduate degree I was destined for office work for the rest of my work life. I wanted a professional career that didn't involve the exchange of money and was useful to society, but I didn't want to spend many years in graduate school.

My mother was the first in her family to go to college. When I was in the sixth grade she got her master's degree in speech and hearing pathology. We lived in Darien, Connecticut where, at that time, being a working mother was highly unusual. My father was a physicist, the principal optical designer on the Hubbell telescope, and had been a librarian during the Depression. Both of my parents had exceptional organizational skills. They taught me to love to read and to enjoy research. Their examples inspired me to get a library science degree. I think it served me well in raising three children, working during some of that time; and the research and organization skills I obtained certainly helped me to become a competent caregiver.

* * *

BARRY:

Before cancer, I was a white-water kayaker. One of the things I noticed was how instinctively better women were at it than men. Men had a tendency to try to muscle their way down a river while women danced along looking for a path. I watched men's muscles give out, saw them getting tired, stiff, klutzy, and inept while the river never quit flowing. Meanwhile the women maintained a grace. Finding the paths where you could dance along seemed to work better than raw muscle power.

Over the past eight years I've tried to treat my ordeal of cancer treatment the way I learned to run a river rapid. I have no evidence to support this strategy. It is just my belief that cancer is a force of nature, like a river, and if I try to fight my cancer as if fighting a rapid the odds of my winning will be poor. Some laugh at the cliché, "go with the flow," but for me cancer invites a Zen perspective.

I have treated my cancer, not as an alien force that has invaded my body, but as a natural process. Some of my own cells are going crazy. We all have potentially cancerous cells in our bodies and we also have corrective measures our bodies can employ to keep them in check. But sometimes these crazy cells get out of control and they can get pretty darn resourceful at beating the treatments we've devised. While I want as much help as I can get in dealing with these recalcitrant cells, in the end I don't want a metaphorical war in my body. For me, eight years of warfare would be draining. I don't have the energy for a lengthy siege, so wherever possible I have chosen to go with the flow and to take whatever measures of life I am allowed. This helps me avoid existential hysteria.

There is a school of thought in the cancer community that emphasizes the importance of positive attitude coupled with encouraging a "survivor" mentality. Published accounts of the experiences of cancer patients must be uplifting and have happy outcomes. Patients are schooled to approach cancer as an enemy and put up a heroic struggle if they are going to prevail. Victory is defined as being cured. But choosing warlike metaphors and adopting a survivor mentality is grounded in fear and has a big downside. If you succumb, is it your fault because you failed to develop the requisite positive attitude?

We have grown accustomed to looking for fault, particularly where cancer is concerned. This perspective has been nurtured in the public mind by the campaign against smoking: "If you smoke you will get lung cancer and it will be your own fault." While this is not always true with lung cancer (a significant percent of lung cancers happen to non-smokers), it is even less true with other types of cancer; but the presumption of fault is not really diminished as far as the general public is concerned. The cancer-free public is fearful of becoming cancer patients; no one can blame them for that—but believing that if you get cancer it's because you have done something wrong, while comforting to the healthy, is both wrong and worthless to those with cancer.

I think cancer patients have enough on their plate without being tarred with the brush of fault, but that's the end game with the positive attitude/survivor strategy. I don't accept that most cancers are the fault of the patient, and I don't buy into the myth that there is a magically successful state of mind which, if you don't achieve this cancer nirvana, makes succumbing your fault. Personally, I'm for trashing the teddy bears, pink ribbons, balloons, and sugar coated attitude pills. I'm for dumping fault. But most of all, I'm for fearing no evil.

Not long ago, one of my oncology nurses, whom I first met in 2006, said that I was different from most of the patients she'd seen in her many years of practice. "How so?" I asked.

"You haven't let cancer own you," she said.

I have thought long on her statement, and she was right. I have cancer, but have never considered myself a survivor. It is a term I don't use to identify who I am. I am wary of coming down with something as a result of my leukemia, which probably lingers in hideaways biding its time to erupt, and I try to be cautious, but I am not going to identify as a survivor. That's not who I am. And as this story unfolds you will see just how that has worked out.

* * *

BONNIE:

Our experiences with cancer began during the thirty-seventh year of our marriage. Barry was bringing home a good income. While female librarians are underpaid, I was productive and content with the work, and I enjoyed my time with my colleagues. Our children were grown so we had the ability to take vacations irrespective of school-year constraints. We regularly practiced yoga, biked, and hiked. We kayaked occasionally. We were busy with family and friends and went out a lot.

As we ushered in the new millennium, only a few of our friends had had major brushes with cancer. There was a smattering of prostate cancer, due primarily to a new and improved PSA test that hit a number of our friends as well as Barry. There were a few diagnoses of breast cancer, but except for our friend, Jean, they'd been caught early and treated. We weren't thinking about our mortality, how one minute you're healthy, or think you are because you're asymptomatic, and how quickly you can find yourself tumbling over the precipice on an accelerating descent into medical hell.

* * *

BARRY:

I was diagnosed with leukemia in July 2005. After nearly a year of confusion and false treatment starts, it was determined that I was in good enough shape to try for a stem cell transplant. Sometimes called a bone marrow transplant, it involves replacing crummy blood with good stuff from someone else. My doctor at Stanford, David Miklos, called it a "hero's cure," by which he meant that if it didn't kill you it just might cure you. On the other hand, if I didn't take this risk, I'd surely be dead in a few years, if not months. It really didn't take much of a hero to go for it when presented this way. All I had to lose was maybe a year and who could tell what the quality of that year might be.

Bonnie and I wrote many of the entries in this book in real time. I was writing to leave a record of my state of mind, as I went through the transplant process, not knowing the outcome. I wasn't trying to prove anything, to play hero or victim. Bonnie was writing to family and friends to tell "our" story about the "battle" we, and especially she, was waging. We were both writing to help us cope. I tended to joke. Bonnie tended to tear up. In many ways, I had the easier job. I just had to survive. Bonnie got to worry and fret over every detail, every dose of medication, and every potential source of infection. In the end, she acquired all the symptoms of post-traumatic stress disorder.

We embarked on this journey together and we are still together. Yet, in many ways each of us had a different experience and our paths often diverged. While I confronted my mortality both intellectually and physically, Bonnie confronted the potential of an early widowhood and both witnessed and experienced a great deal of suffering. In retrospect, I am not sure which path I'd have chosen if I had the choice. After all, I am here to write this, and so is she, but we are not the same people we were in 2005 when this ordeal began. This is both a story about cancer and the story of a relationship under stress, experiencing the same adversity differently, and how we received many gifts that allowed us to live our lives while coping with it.

CHAPTER ONE

Asymptomatic

BARRY:

Asymptomatic—Posted June 9, 2006

It is July 25, 2005. I am slumped at a desk piled with legal papers, yellow pads, and books studded with Post-its. The reminder on my Outlook pops up to warn me my annual check-up is in one hour. I sigh deeply.

This annual check-up thing is Bonnie's idea. She claims it is something you're supposed to do when you turn fifty. I am sixty now and feeling great. I don't need to see a doctor. We just returned from a vacation in New Zealand where we put thirty-five miles of turquoise seawater under our kayak in three days. We topped that off with another thirty-five miles of hiking on the Milford Track in rain and mud, scrambling over rocks and roots. What more do you need to tell you you're fit and healthy?

I'm a busy trial lawyer, a job that requires wits, energy, and constant attention to details. It is a younger man's job and that's my identity. There are plenty of other items on my Outlook—up-coming depositions that want preparing, some witness interviews, hustling a new case. A client or two is due for a handholding session in the critical weeks before pending trials. A couple of phone calls are screaming for immediate attention and there is a rough draft of a memo that needs some proofing before a rapidly approaching hearing date. Any one of those tasks is more important than spending two or three hours in an annual check-up that I don't need.

I exhale with the kind of annoyance one has when ripped from a productive chain of thought. "Get it together," I tell myself. I begin to search my desk for the stuff I might need while cooling my heels in a doctor's waiting room. I toss a draft of that legal memo into my briefcase along with my cell phone, car keys, sunglasses, and a novel that I am reading, should I decide to play hooky from the billable hour racket. I want to give myself choices for the boring foreplay of the doctor's waiting room.

"I'm going out for about three hours," I say to Cheryl, our receptionist. "Tell whoever calls that they can either call back late this afternoon or leave a message and I'll return their calls when I get back."

I wore out my paddling gloves in New Zealand and want to get another pair on the way home. I make a quick call to REI to find out when they close. I have until six o'clock. And it looks like Bonnie has us set up for a screening at the Jewish Film Festival for 8:30. Things are going to be tight but manageable.

I know it was a sunny day. I know that more from the journey back than from the drive out. On the way out there I can't say I notice much. It is almost a straight shot down California—no brains required. I am driving by rote, editing my memo in my head.

When I visit my doctor I like to try to park my car on Parker. That's the name of the street. I think it's good luck if I can be a parker on Parker. I have a small car, a Prius and that's good karma. I find a parking space in front of 50 Parker. A Chinese client once told me that fifty is a lucky number. Good karma, good luck. Today's my day all right.

I'm a little early but I feel like jogging the half block to the doctor's office. It's only a half block and I won't work up a sweat or anything. I've been sitting around all day and just want to burn off a little energy.

Doctor Parmer's waiting room is empty—another good sign. I won't have to wait; I'm on a roll. I could convert those edits I made in my head onto the draft, but I'm feeling a little liberated so I decide to read a bit of the novel. I've barely finished a page of it when Dr. Parmer opens the door to the waiting room.

"Barry," he says. He's holding my chart in his hand. Doctor Parmer is only about five years younger than me, but he's managed to retain a perpetual youthfulness. You can count on one hand the strands of gray in his full head of black hair. His skin is smooth and gives the impression that he is worry-free and I like that. He talks to you, not at you. I like that too. That's why he's my doctor.

"Hi Bill," I say as I bounce out of my chair. "How's it going?"

He gives me a wan smile. He must be having a bad day. He ushers me into one of his examination rooms and tells me to have a seat on the examination table. Usually one of his assistants does that. She walks in, takes my blood pressure and temperature and writes that down. I wait there for a bit before I see Bill again. I barely process the difference. Bill takes a seat at his little desk and flips open the chart.

"I've got all your tests back," he says in a voice low enough that I have to supplement my hearing by reading his lips. "Everything looks good except for your white blood count."

"So," I shrug. "What's that all about?"

"Well, Barry," he begins. He wants to look at me but is having some trouble maintaining eye contact. "It looks like you've got early stage leukemia, or maybe it's lymphoma, but we think it's CLL."

Did he say "we?" "You mean you've had a second opinion?"

"Pathology looks at these things before they send them on to me," he explains.

I don't know squat about leukemia or lymphoma. They're just words that I see on a poster in the BART trains on the way to work, "Living with Lymphoma." There's a healthy looking guy and a little kid in the graphic. There are posters like that for every problem. Who pays attention?

"What is this CLL?" I ask, even though I'm not sure I'm processing things well anymore. I wish I had someone along with me who could do that kind of work for me.

"CLL is short for chronic lymphocytic leukemia," he says, as if translating letters into multi-syllabic jargon constitutes an explanation. I know what he is doing. I'm a professional too and in times like this we tend to seek refuge in our techno-babble.

"So what's it mean?" I ask. I want him to give me a prognosis.

"It's not as bad as it sounds," he says. "I don't want to scare you. We've got a lot of tests to do."

"Come on, Bill," I say. I must have sounded annoyed because he anted up.

"Well, if what you've got is indolent, the statistics say ten to thirteen years median life expectancy. If it's aggressive, then three to five."

It sounds like a sentence for robbery. I want to plea bargain.

"But those numbers don't mean very much," he continues. "Everybody's different and every day they're coming up with new therapies. Leukemia's a growth industry. We're seeing an epidemic of it among baby boomers. We don't know why, but everybody's thinking environment. And Genentech's got this drug, Rituxan, which seems to be working. But it's only been out about five years, so you can see that it makes the stats somewhat sketchy."

"But I feel great, Bill. I don't feel anything," I say, pleading my case.

"You're what they call asymptomatic, Barry," he explains. "You could be that way for quite a while, years and years."

"Or not."

"Or not. They're also moving ahead with stem cell therapies," he says. "They're getting good results. A couple of years from now we could be there."

"Stem cells," I repeat. "What Bush and his gang of religious crazies want to flush down the toilet instead of giving to research. I guess it's getting personal between me and him now."

Bill wants to laugh. I can see that, but he can't. We go through a pro forma examination. I'm thinking three to five, ten to thirteen. I find myself rooting for ten to thirteen. My father, who had polio when he was a child, is nearly ninety. My mother, who was sickly all of her life, lived to eighty-six. I'll be lucky to pick up a social security check. I don't hear another word he says over the next hour.

I leave the office in a daze, walking slowly, as if I am elderly. Outside I notice that it is sunny. I feel the breeze blowing in from the west and I can even smell the salt in the air. The clouds are moving fast and there are yellow lilies, or something—my flower identification skills stink—waving back and forth in a freshly planted bed in front of number 50.

I get into the Prius and close the door on my coat. I'm crazed and pull out of the space heedless of fuel economy. I make a left on Geary, roll down the window and yell, "Fuck man, you asshole!" at some hapless fool in the car that just pulled in front of me. And I don't stop there. "Asshole, what is it you don't understand about the word 'Stop?'" He gives me the finger. I pull up alongside of him and give him one back. Today I'm bullet- proof, I say to myself. I'm Clark Gable and I frankly don't give a damn. "Fuck you!" I tell him, this time without the sign language. He can see I'm a lunatic and he accelerates out of my life.

I'm not going back to work today. Everything there is about money, and suddenly I don't need so much of it. I have to call Cheryl though and tell her.

"Shit. Fuck, shit, shit, shit, fuck." I've forgotten my briefcase in Bill's examination room. Do I want it? Do I need it? I can go home and spend the day actually living, thinking about myself, and not whether someone is going to recover six months' back rent or receive an award of treble damages. I don't want to hear some whiny client or some self-important adversary spouting bullshit that he made up on the crapper and is laying on me since he thought it sounded plausible. There really is no call that has to be made. So what if that memo won't be my best work? Who'll notice in two months? After the case is over and the file goes off to its own little storage cemetery, no one will ever think about it again. Maybe that's about to happen to me too. It gives "important" a new meaning.

But I have another call to make. I do a U-turn on Geary and suddenly I'm the one who doesn't understand the meaning of "Stop." I discover that this time I cannot be a parker on Parker, but there is half a space plus a little bit of bus stop that will do for a moment. I run because I still can.

I decide not to wait for the elevator and bound up the stairs two at a time. My briefcase is waiting at the receptionist's desk. At least I am polite to her. But before I leave I open the briefcase and toss the novel on the table with all the magazines. I can't finish it; I can't read that page that I was reading less than two hours ago, before my life was turned upside down. It's a good book, but for me it's become bad luck. I can remember lots of things about that day but not the title of that book, or the author, or even what it was about.

I sit on the concrete wall outside the office building and speed dial Bonnie's number. "Hi," I say.

"What's the matter?" she says."

"What?" I say.

"I can hear something in your voice," she says.

"I had my exam," I say. "The good news is that I'm asymptomatic."

* * *

BONNIE:

There is nothing memorable about Monday, July 25, 2005, the day everything changes in our lives, until late afternoon. I am sitting at my desk at work when Barry calls. I'm aware that he's having a physical with Dr. Parmer that afternoon because I've reminded him to make the copay with our credit card so my insurance records will be straight and I'll be able to have the least amount of contact with our insurance company. The first thing he says is they wouldn't take a credit card. But there's something in his voice. The second thing he tells me is that he's been diagnosed with CLL (chronic lymphocytic leukemia). I'm usually pretty chatty on the phone but that bombshell leaves me speechless.

The diagnosis is a result of Barry's rising white blood count. Neither of us has ever heard of CLL before, but I quickly learn that normal is 4,000–11,000. Barry's is at 12,000 and has been rising over the last couple of years. Dr. Parmer has reassured him that CLL is an indolent disease and that people live for decades with it. Nevertheless, he's referring Barry to a hematologist.

I'm the regional librarian for an engineering firm. One of its specialties is retrofitting buildings to meet current earthquake codes. For the owner of endangered buildings, we are like doctors. The firm's assignment is to make the building safe and healthy. One of my jobs is to locate materials the engineers need to do their job. They task me to search the building codes for when it was built and to find reference materials the engineers think might be relevant to cure the structure's deficiencies. My instinct is to apply these same research skills to my husband and to get the full scoop on this CLL. I immediately call my cousin Rick who is a pathologist in L.A. He agrees with Dr. Parmer's view of CLL and that is reassuring.

At first Barry wants to keep his diagnosis a secret. He seems to think that if we don't tell anyone, it will mean that he doesn't really have cancer. This is hard for me; I'm the one who finds it comforting to share and I guess my face is an open book. The next night we are having dinner with dear friends and one, Judy, can tell something is wrong, so I tell her. Once the dam is broken there is no turning back. We tell our children, close family, and then some very close friends. The news gets around among our circle of friends, and after that, there is no point in secrecy.

* * *

BARRY:

Bonnie hits the Internet like the asteroid that crashed into the earth, extinguishing the dinosaurs. In this case, the dinosaur is our old life. The Internet has no filters for this kind of stuff. Much is anecdotal and horrific. There is venting. There is anger. There is misinformation. And then there are medical studies that are incomprehensible and require subscriptions to esoteric journals. We learn more than we want to know and start to go crazy. Meanwhile, I have been referred to an oncologist who "specializes in blood cancers." That sounds pretty good to me, until much later I discover that specializing in blood cancers is the modern equivalent of a general practitioner.

Bonnie joins me for my first appointment, as she will do for nearly every appointment and procedure that will follow. She brings along a list of many questions and a yellow pad to write everything down. I have nothing. I know there is no point in relying on my powers of comprehension or recall. After Dr. Parmer said "CLL," what I heard was like that Gary Larsen cartoon: "What you say to Fido and what Fido hears." I am Fido. I hear: blah, blah, blah, leukemia, blah, blah, lymphoma. Blah, blah, blah, blah, three years. Blah, blah, five years. Blah, blah, ten years. Blah, fourteen years. Blah blah. And I retain even less.

My first oncology appointment is about three weeks after Dr. Parmer delivered his diagnosis. With some kinds of cancer, this would be a long interval, but since it is CLL, which in most cases is indolent, there should be nothing immediate to panic over. I am asymptomatic and the experience is cloaked in surrealism. It's as if I were an actor playing the role of cancer patient in a daytime soap.

Still, as I open the door to his office for that premiere visit, I can't subdue my anxieties. I have this vision of Auguste Rodin's masterpiece, "The Gates of Hell," and I see myself becoming one those lost souls falling, flailing, grasping helplessly and hopelessly into the abyss that is the inevitable fate of the damned. I envision my first oncologist as a sort of Cerberus, the guard dog of hell. I feel fine but fear that I will never be allowed to leave.

Dr. T appears to have a thriving practice. The waiting area is full. Some patients seem to be dozing. Others are listlessly flipping through dated periodicals. I take a seat opposite a young woman who is completely hairless and has not bothered with the scarves or caps many women use. Her skin is both flawless and translucent, drawn tightly to reveal high cheekbones and a finely chiseled jawline. She has a small upturned nose and large blue eyes, and she reminds me of a space alien. She's been beautiful in her life, and the evidence of that beauty remains, despite the toll her cancer has taken. From time to time I look over the top of my magazine and sneak a glance, imagining her "before." I'm saddened. She is so young. When it is time for her to see the doctor, she grips the arm of her companion and walks slowly away. I will return to Dr. T's offices many times over the next eight months, but I'll never see her again.

Up to now, whenever I've thought of cancer patients, the images have been of older folks. I've not conjured up young people who've been stricken before they've had a chance to live. I am sixty and I've had a pretty eventful life. I've been able to do nearly everything I've wanted to do. I've had a wonderful long-term marriage. I've got three loving daughters. I've traveled and had my share of thrills. I've achieved a modicum of professional success and recognition. Next month I'll receive an award as AIDS Legal Referral Panel Lawyer of the Year for 2005. But these kids, who deserve to have long lives ahead of them, probably won't—at least not most of them. They will have to cram an entire lifetime into a few short years, or maybe less. Their days will pass with anticipatory regret because they know most of their hopes and dreams will be unfulfilled. In a flash I recognize I am experiencing survivor's guilt. I have already lived twice their lives, and according to Dr. Palmer's prognosis, I am likely to survive them. I don't know them. I don't know what they are like, what they believe. I haven't a clue whether they are serious or frivolous, whether they are racists or anti-Semites. But I realize that I don't care whether, in another life, I would have liked to punch them out or take them for lovers. This sadness upon seeing the young ones never passes.

Before I get to see Dr. T, they do a blood draw. The procedure is uncomfortable. I do not have easily accessible veins. This will prove to be a problem throughout my treatment. Only the most skilled phlebotomists seem consistently able to insert the needle on the first try. I've had experienced RNs give up after three or four attempts on each arm. I can leave one of those draw experiences with tracks like a heroin addict.

The assistant who draws the blood shakes the vial. It looks to me dark and very red and healthy. It crosses my mind that maybe it was all a big mistake and they are going to find that the spike in WBC was due to some infection that has now passed out of my body. There's a chance, I say to myself, this draw will show I'm okay. I will make my escape. She shakes up the contents and inserts it into a box-like machine that makes mechanical noises to assure us it knows what it is doing. The thing then spits out a report on a sheet of paper as if it were sticking out its tongue at me. She looks at it with a blank expression and says only, "The doctor will be with you in a moment."

Dr. T invites us into his office after another wait. It's a cluttered place. There are a lot of papers on his desk, books on his shelves and his computer is open to some report, I think. He has all the expected certificates on the wall and the obligatory pictures of his family—his robust wife and kids engaged in recreational activity—to demonstrate that he has another, more human, more familiar life than simply passing out death sentences. I wonder how he does it—how any oncologist does it—day after day meeting people with basically one objective: to prolong the inevitable while dashing false hopes and moderating the pain.

Dr. T gives me a brief physical examination. He says that he has not yet made a diagnosis. He knows that Dr. Parmer thinks I have CLL but it is too soon to tell. He is going to send some of my blood to the California Pacific Medical Center lab for analysis. I will have to come back in a couple of weeks to discuss the results. Oh, and yes, my WBC is now 14,000, up 2000 in only a few weeks.

That news bursts my bubble. I'm not going to walk out of there with a clean bill of health. "It was 11 or 12,000 only a couple of weeks ago," I say with a hint of panic.

Dr. T shrugs. "A change of a couple thousand is within the margin of error."

Bonnie has some questions. I can't remember a single one—or a single one of his answers.

* * *

BONNIE:

We meet with Dr. T. for the first time on August 15. The wait is interminable. (We soon find this to be the case for all our visits with him. Sometimes there aren't even enough seats.) The routine, we learn, is to get basic blood work done before seeing him.

Dr. T. greets us warmly, which I find comforting. He sits down at his cluttered desk and begins perusing the blood work results. After a while he tells us he agrees with the CLL diagnosis, but he wants to schedule extensive blood work, a PET-CT scan and a bone marrow biopsy.

* * *

BARRY:

Two weeks later we return to Dr. T's offices. In the waiting room the cast of characters are different, but very much in the same condition. I can't help wondering whether any of the crew from a fortnight ago is no longer with us. After a while, the technician appears, calls out my name, and escorts me back for another blood draw. I am still not used to them, although within a year it will become absentminded foreplay in a treatment ritual. As she runs her eyes over my WBC results, I try to engage her in small talk, hoping to catch an adjustment in her expression, but she is on to tricks like that. She does this perhaps twenty times a day. I'm betting a lot of patients try some ploy to get her to reveal the results.

This afternoon, Dr. T has some real news, the lab results. They've done chromatography, flow cytometry, fancy lab kinds of stuff. He shows us a sheaf of papers attesting that they've done the work and has a copy for us to take home. "The bottom line," he explains, "is that they can't tell for sure what you have."

"You mean it's not CLL?" Bonnie asks. My question exactly.

"That's still a possibility," Dr. T nods. "But it also could be a B-cell lymphoma or even WM, Waldenström's macroglobulinemia." He looks at us as if we are supposed to be in the know about WM.

"What the hell is Waldenström's macroglobulinemia?" I blurt, probably mispronouncing the condition.

"It's rare and indolent. That means a slow-growing, non-Hodgkin lymphoma, also called lymphoplasmacytic lymphoma," he says, looking up from his clutter to make sure I get it. "It affects the white blood cells, the B cells." He looks back down at the printout from today's WBC and raises his eyebrows. "It's close to 16,000 today."

"I'm going up a thousand a week," I say with a hint of desperation. "But I don't feel any different. I feel fine."

"I have patients whose counts are over 200,000 and they feel fine too," he reassures me.

I do a rough calculation. Maybe I've got a hundred and eighty-four weeks then, I think. Nearly four years.

Bonnie, who has been doing online research says, "The B cells, they're the ones that carry your immunities, right? When they don't work right, you lose your body's natural protections against infections."

Dr. T, it seems, would like to explain things in a more complicated way. Perhaps, that's what he is doing, because Bonnie is writing things down on her yellow pad and nodding as if she understands what he is saying. All I get is they are still going to be testing and trying to figure out what I have.

I get my first inkling that Dr. T is in over his head. Otherwise, for me it's a lot of blah blah. But I'm also ready to go with Waldenström. I heard the words "indolent" and "slow growing" and if I'm going to have a blood cancer, I'm ready to opt for that kind.

BONNIE:

At our next appointment, Dr. T. told us he was puzzled by the results of Barry's extensive blood work. Now, he did not think it was CLL; perhaps it was something called Waldenström's macroglobulinemia. There were chromosomal abnormalities, he said. He needed to do a biopsy.

Of course, I went on the Internet as soon as I got home to read up on Waldenström's. It didn't look too bad, but being web research, it was not completely reassuring and somewhat anecdotal. Internet research can freak you out if you are not careful. As a reference librarian, I'm very aware of the problem. People tend to post their horror stories, and if you aren't careful you can easily get hysterical. WM had some of those stories, but as with everything about cancer, the distinctions are the key. One person's horror may be another's salvation.

* * *

BARRY:

That weekend we go hiking at Pt. Reyes with our friends Geoff and Mary. We head out to the Elk Reservation, taking a trail that runs along a point of land on the west side of Tomales Bay for four miles or so. The day is clear with an unclouded horizon at the outer limits of potential visibility. Looking back over my shoulder, I can see far beyond the Golden Gate, past Pillar Point to the hazy front of the Santa Cruz Mountains. Ridges of cobalt waves, seeming like mere ripples from our vantage point on the high cliffs assault the coast in neat well-formed sets. I used to be a surfer and get that old longing to be on a board, dropping into a face as smooth and ripple free as polished marble, making a turn, hunkering down and slip-sliding across a watery wall of glass. All along the shore I know folks are surfing without a care or concern for mortality, just as I have done.

I'd hiked this trail several times before my diagnosis, but I remember little of those details. This time though, nearly every step is indelibly etched into my memory. I can feel the wind and smell the ocean salt as it whips across the landscape. I see the grass bending. On the hills behind me, small groups of does cluster around their antlered rulers who have won the right to mate with a harem through brute force. Far away are a group of loser males peering enviously at the alphas. I see them all. I see everything and internalize its essence. Mary, Geoff, Bonnie, and I joke and banter as we hike along with brisk energized strides. We are pictures of health, in our prime. I point my face into the wind, raise a fist in defiance and scream: "Fuck you Waldenström, whomever the hell you are."

The wind swallows my protest.

* * *

BONNIE:

A few weeks later Barry has a biopsy. While Barry is still drugged up, Dr. T. chillingly declares, "If this was CLL, I'd understand these abnormalities."

Then, in late September, Dr. T changed the diagnosis yet again. Now he was telling us it appeared Barry had a low grade lymphoma. And maybe, he speculated, there were two blood cancers at the same time. "I think we'd best get a consultation," he said as he perused Barry's paperwork. "You have really good insurance. I can send you anywhere."

Three diagnoses in two months! We were reeling. What was next?

Thinking out loud Dr. T tells us that Stanford is the place to go for blood cancers and he recommends Dr. Steven Coutre, who is both a CLL-specialist and also a Waldenström's specialist. "He's Talmudic," our Chinese-American doctor says. We like that.

CHAPTER TWO

What's Happening?

BARRY:

Stanford University Cancer Center is a teaching hospital where they perform clinical trials and are up on all the latest treatments. Getting an appointment with Dr. Coutre, I'm told, can be as difficult as getting admitted to college. You've got to earn it with something unusual. Apparently I fit the bill. Just my luck, I am thinking, to have a rare, unusual, and difficult to diagnose blood cancer, instead of one of those run-of-the mill kinds that everybody knows how to treat. While I was being facetious when I rued my fate, little did I know just how lucky this confluence of circumstances would be for me.

So, in the perverse world of cancer, I am lucky. I have really great insurance and "lucky" to have a rare, ambiguous condition that piques the interest of researchers at one of the premier medical research universities in the entire world, which happens to be right in my back yard. I'm lucky to get an early appointment with a stellar specialist in B-cell blood disorders. I'm extra-lucky to have a wife who knows how to be my advocate and ask the right questions. For now, I'll leave it at that because, as you may guess, the list gets a whole lot longer.

The Stanford Cancer Center in Palo Alto sits right next to the hospital, about midway between the upscale shopping center that the University runs as a profit center and the undergraduate campus. The Cancer Center is new, sparkling, and resonating with live harp music. On my first visit, I noticed helicopters landing on the roof of the hospital as if it was the U.S. embassy in Saigon, circa 1975. It seems they are shutting down public hospitals in Santa Clara County because California voters don't distinguish between public health and pork. That leaves Stanford, which actually costs the public more than if they'd bothered to fund a public hospital, particularly when you factor in the chopper delivery system. Perversely there's a certain egalitarian twist to the scheme. The same department could be treating the jewel-encrusted arm candy of a Silicon Valley CEO one minute and the next an East Palo Alto junkie in cuffs with a pair of armed deputies as escorts.

Dr. Coutre is another one of those youngish looking docs who must be older but seems to have access to the same secret fountain of youthfulness as Dr. Parmer. We meet him in a windowless examination room. There is a computer that can log on to a database containing my records. It's just a consultation; but whatever it is that Dr. T has sent along seems to have been scanned in. Dr. Coutre appears to be familiar with my condition already. He asks questions. Bonnie does a lot of the answering for me and asks questions back.

I can't recall a word of the conversation except that the diagnosis remains unclear. I have these markers. CD3 or CD5 that may be clonal T lymphocytes—or maybe not. They don't seem out of the normal range. I have something going on with my B cell markers CD19, CD22 and CD54. He'll recommend to Dr. T that more studies are necessary. "When's your next appointment with him?"

"Early December. Should I move it up?"

Dr. Coutre thinks that maybe they'll need that kind of time to process the information the new tests will show. He sets me up for more blood work right then and there. He'll keep in touch with Dr. T.

"What about Waldenström?" I ask, almost hopefully, clinging to the adjective that Dr. T used to describe it: "indolent."

Coutre shakes his head. "No. I don't think it is that."

I'm disappointed, even though I don't have enough knowledge to know whether I should be or not.

I look over at Bonnie and read her mind. "There's that glass half-empty again," she's thinking. "What kinds of treatments are available for CLL and B-cell lymphoma?" she asks.

Dr. Coutre rattles off some long-winded names of chemo treatments that come down to some form of CHOP thing where you lose your hair and feel like shit. There's rituximab, which he describes as a monoclonal antibody, a kind of treatment that targets those blood markers he's so concerned about. He tells us rituximab gloms onto the cells with those markers and prevents them from replicating. It manages to single out the bad guys without killing all the innocent civilians, like old-line chemo does.

I'm thinking, ah that old targeted strike sales pitch. No collateral damage. No hair loss. A lot less sickness.

"And if we can get you into remission," he says, "then you might be eligible for a transplant. It's a dangerous procedure—some people die during it—but if it works, it can be a complete cure. You come out of it with a whole new blood supply that's healthy. But that's way down the road. First we've got to figure out what you've got."

So as we walk out of there, Bonnie is talking about how they've got a whole lot of treatments, any one of which just might work and they even have one that could cure me completely. She's hopeful. I come out of there thinking: they may never figure out what I have; they're going to give me shit that will make me sick and hairless, and after that they're going to put me through a procedure that will kill me. What the fuck is she so upbeat about?

* * *

BONNIE:

It is mid-October 2005 when we drive down to Stanford for the first time, little realizing how familiar that drive would soon become.

Steven Coutre works at the Stanford Cancer Center—he's not in private practice. The exam rooms are small, windowless, and impersonal. There's nothing on the walls—no degrees, awards or family photos—to divert your attention from the doctor. Despite being youngish and low key he speaks with authority and exudes confidence.

Dr. Coutre thinks Barry might have CLL, and definitely rules out Waldenstrom's. He mentions it also could be a B-cell lymphoproliferative disorder (whatever that is) and he feels like it's an indolent disease. He does not recommend treatment. I am relieved, but Barry is beginning to feel frustrated that nothing is happening. He wants to be proactive. We would live to regret that tendency.

Over the next couple of months, Barry's white blood count keeps rising; but that doesn't stop us from going on with our lives as if he were completely healthy. Over Christmas we travel to Mexico with our daughter and very close friends, Gus, Ellen, and Hope, not realizing the risks we are taking by traveling to a third-world country. Barry has an appointment scheduled with Dr. T. in early January. I decide not to go because it is always the same—nothing happening. In retrospect, I should have gone. At that appointment, Barry's white blood count was 35,000. It had doubled in less than six months, and he'd had it. He demanded that we get proactive.

Dr. T. recommended treatment with Rituxan, a monoclonal antibody treatment for Lymphoma. "We give it out like water," Barry reported Dr. T telling him, and he jumped at the opportunity to give it a try. When he told me, I was not as enthusiastic, but decided to get with the program and be supportive. His first treatment was scheduled for early February.

* * *

BARRY:

Before I know it, it is early January 2006 and time for my next meeting with Dr. T. By this point, I'm under no illusions that I'm going to get good news, or any news at all, replacing such expectations with Dante's imagined admonition at the Gates of Hell: "All hope abandon, ye who enter here."

My expectations of a glass half empty are fulfilled. There is still no diagnosis. Now Dr. T is leaning in the direction of a B-cell lymphoma, and along with all hope I might as well strike the "indolent" from the description of whatever I have. My WBC is now around 34,000.

"A doubling of your WBC in three months," Dr. T says, "means that the disease is aggressive." He shrugs when I ask for a suggestion as to treatment.

"What about Rituxan?" I ask.

"We give it out around here like water," he says. "It works almost all the time."

I'm anxious to do something besides waiting around and watching my white blood count heading into outer space. "Well, why don't we try it?"

He meets my eyes with a stare like a deer in my headlights. "We could do that."

I'm half expecting him to shrug. He's letting me decide my treatment. He doesn't know what to do. I wonder what he'd say if I asked him to give me a prescription for morphine. "I'd like to give it a shot," I tell him.

We decide that it can wait another six weeks. Bonnie has a trip planned at the end of January. Her women friends are having a birthday bash at a spa just across the border in Mexico. She wonders whether she ought to cancel. I want her to go. I don't want to play the guilt card just yet—there'll be plenty of time for that, I'm sure.

"I want to go to Hawaii, anyway," I say. I have friends there, on the Big Island, near Puna, just south of Hilo. Puna is one of those vestigial remnants of the by-gone era we have come to call the Sixties. I know the era well. To Robin Williams's sardonic statement, "If you can remember the Sixties you weren't there," I say: "Au contraire Robin, I can and do re-member it. I was there." Actually, there are some things I'd like to forget, but that's another story.

I've seen pictures of the place I have in mind and it strikes me as the next generation after the "little grass shack." I've got a bit of a hippie streak in me and I'm set up to blow my mind in paradise. I'm still asymptomatic, except for my mental condition, and I know when I get there my friend Dean will point me in the right direction to acquire a homegrown remedy for that.

In a few days, I am drinking in the orchard-laden air along with a big mug of Kona coffee and rolling down the road to Puna. Half way up the Mauna Loa volcano, I enter the national park and the tropics disappear into a haze of fog, rain, and holy shit, a snow flurry. I'm wearing a tee shirt and shorts and am forced to close the windows in my rental car, turn on the heat and defroster. After a bit of winter, I crest a hill and sprawling below me is a broad plateau. The lower slope of the great shield volcano is basking in golden sunlight and in the distance a bejeweled turquoise Pacific. What an amazing world we live in, I tell myself, in awe of the scene. For a moment I wonder, am I going to get to miss it? Spend my last months lying on a hospital bed, tubes putting stuff in and taking stuff out, machines running my vitals twenty-four/seven? Or will it just be over in a flash? Then, I put it out of my mind. I am here now. I have all my marbles. I can swim and hike, do everything I ever could. Screw the WBC and the Rituxan. Tomorrow can wait forever as far as I'm concerned.

Dean's place is in the jungle, off a dirt road with ruts and potholes that require a lot of weaving and braking. I'm sure the rental contract is voided if I hang the car up on one of the craters that pock this thoroughfare. To my left, giant, erratic waves aggressively dash themselves heedlessly onto cliffs of gray pumice with the consistency of Swiss cheese, sending aloft towering mists of saltwater and creating ephemeral rainbows. Dean tells me that this mist, as beautiful as it is, is a nemesis capable of rotting a cor-rugated iron roof in a couple of years. You can forget it if you expect any appliance to outlast the manufacturer's warranty. It is a metaphor for life.

He has acquired his house and five lush, moist acres, just across the road from the ocean for—well I'm not selling real estate, so I'll let it pass with an ambiguous, "song." His jungle conjures up *Heart of Darkness*. He constantly has to cut back the vegetation, he tells me, or else it will overgrow the entire place in no time. That night, some sort of drum circle thing is going on back beyond the clearing that he maintains for his living space. "They do that every night," he explains with a defeatist shake of his head. I hear footprints patter across the metal roof above my head, and look up.

"Rats or ferrets or some such creatures," he says resignedly.

Yes, *Heart of Darkness*. The place requires constant work—exhausting work—the kind that helps you fall asleep despite the natives drumming into the wee hours and the rodents prancing above your head. All your worldly possessions rot out in a matter of months. The price he paid now makes more sense.

For a blissful week, Dean and I hike in the great craters of Mauna Loa, browse at the farmer's market outside of Puna, swim in the warm pools heated by volcanic activity, snorkel in the saltwater ponds that interrupt the vast stretch of hardened lava between jungle and ocean, and take in the nude optional beach. I visit the Hawaii Tropical Botanical Gardens just north of Hilo and explore the small authentic Hawaiian villages on the northeast side of the island. I shop for orchids for Bonnie's birthday. That week, I do not have cancer.

CHAPTER THREE

Changing Doctors in Mid-Stream

BARRY:

A few days after I return from Hawaii, I get my first view of the suite where the patients of Dr. T's group received their chemotherapy infusions. Beyond the waiting area oversized recliners line the walls of several rooms, each paired with something that looks like a coat rack on wheels with a control box at waist level. Wherever a patient occupies one of those chairs, transparent bottles or clear bags of liquids hang from the racks, dripping into his or her arm the medications that could save them, prolong their lives, or just as easily end them. It is quiet, save for slight hums and low murmurs of equipment occasionally punctuated by startling mechanical bleeps that usually mean a bottle has been drained.

In early February 2006 when I receive my first infusion of Rituxan, my WBC is 44,000. I settle in one of the big chairs. A nurse comes by with a bottle of liquid, reads my name off the bag and asks if I am that person. I nod, and then she recites from the label that I'm about to get some amount of rituximab, presumably to give me the opportunity to protest and tell her: "Hey, I'm here for a full body massage. This must be a mistake." It turns out that some nurse failed to go through this ritual once (probably more than once). The patient got the wrong stuff and dropped dead. Less than a year later, I'll have my own experience with that kind of error.

"You might feel nauseous," she warns as she sticks an intravenous needle into my arm and turns the spigot. But I feel nothing at all—except a bit of hopefulness. They give out rituximab like water, I'm thinking. It's the latest thing in cancer treatment, a monoclonal antibody not the old-line chemo, a huge profit center for Genentech. Obviously, a lot of patients with B-cell lymphoma benefit from it. Why should I be any different?

The treatment plan is to pour a bottle of Rituxan into my blood once each week for four straight weeks. I'll begin each session with a CBC, a complete blood count that includes what, in my mind, comes to symbolize the gold standard for determining disease progression, the WBC. So when I arrive for the second treatment I'm going to get an inkling of how effective rituximab might be on my particular brand of leukemia, lymphoma, Waldenström's, or whatever.

The following week, I'm anxious, excited. This stuff is just going to work. I know it. The nurse makes a copy of the printout. 33,000. Down eleven. I'm back to where I was in December. Not too shabby. I was hoping for more but it's a start. Next week I could be down in the low twenties, maybe September–October levels.

Dr. T meets with us. Yes, it looks like it's working. He's not projecting euphoria at the results but he's not morose. "We won't really know how well this stuff is working until several weeks have passed after the last treatment," he cautions. "See you next week." And he's off to bring tidings to the next patient.

* * *

BONNIE:

Dr. T's oncology practice has its own chemotherapy suite right next door to the medical office. Once you get past the waiting room, there are about eight chemo chairs and a few private rooms. Most people sit in the chemo chairs while the nurses administer the chemo, which can take any time from an hour to half a day.

We had been told that Barry could experience some fairly severe side effects from the Rituxan after the first hour of the drip. After Barry was seated, I overheard one of the nurses say to her colleague, "Now the shit's going to hit the fan." Not a good start.

* * *

BARRY:

I've arranged to give up my pricey office in the downtown financial district. I am a trial attorney and lawsuits take two, three, even five or six years to get to trial, depending on their complexity. I'm telling my clients that I will have to refer them to new lawyers and I'm telling prospective new clients I can't take their cases. I can't count on being around at the end of my cases and it's not fair to them to have to pay a new lawyer to get up to speed two years from now. So, income is plummeting and I don't want to blow my reserves on high rent or other expenses that have no promise of a return. We begin to construct a home office, which will make it easier for me to work in the event I become less mobile, and which is a lot cheaper.

I'm not going to like losing the collegiality of an office environment. I'm not happy about the prospect of benching myself. San Francisco is full of hustling lawyers. You take yourself out of play, especially when you're sixty, and you don't have great prospects for making a comeback. I have to alter my headset. I'm going to be a retired lawyer, whether I like it or not.

"Look you've been talking about retiring for years," Bonnie says. "Now this is just the kick in the pants you need to get you to do it."

I don't want a kick in the pants. I favor procrastination, grouching, grousing, and inertia. But not when it comes to those white blood cells, I don't. The next week can come none too soon for me. We're being proactive now. I like that. I want to stop this disease progression before it gets out of hand and I start getting symptoms.

Week three: I'm hooked up again and the juice is dripping down the tube and into my arm. The test results are in. I hold my breath. I scan the printout. I read it a couple of times to make certain it isn't a mistake. 30,000. I didn't even get into the twenties with the second infusion. This does not look good. I'm devastated. Dr. T reminds me that we really won't know the results for at least another three weeks. I should stay positive.

This is bullshit. These infusions are seven or eight grand a piece. I'm not getting my insurance company's money's worth, I can tell you that. "All hope abandon, ye who enter here."

"So what's next if rituximab doesn't work?" I ask.

"Chemo," says Dr. T. "We'll see. Let's cross that bridge when we come to it."

I can see that bridge in the near distance. The approach is straight and narrow. There are no off ramps between it and me. I just know we're going to cross it. Whenever somebody uses that shopworn bridge metaphor, it's code for: "I don't know what the hell to do next and I just hope I don't have to make a decision." Dr. T is avoiding the inevitable, I'm thinking. It might be nice if you'd get that diagnosis together, I want to say. Maybe that will help us figure out what to do. But okay, we still have another bottle of seven grand to consume.

It's March now. I'm still feeling fine, physically, but becoming increasingly desperate mentally. No diagnosis. No prognosis. No effective treatment. I might as well be living in the Dark Ages for all modern medicine is worth. I'm starting to build up some resentment toward the medical establishment.

They stick me with the IV and start bottle number four. They hand Bonnie the CBC results. She reads the paper like a judge reading a verdict silently before handing it to the clerk to read aloud. She passes it on to me. This time it is in line with my diminishing expectations. Back up to 33,000. Back to where I was after bottle number one. It is UP. Not only didn't the last bottle have a positive effect, the white blood army is on the march. Like in the Russian Civil War—the Whites against the Reds. But unlike Russia circa 1922, the Czarists are winning. The counterrevolution is upon us. To paraphrase Senator Lloyd Bentsen's classic remark about JFK during his VP debate with Dan Quayle: I know Stalin, and whatever Rituxan is, it certainly isn't Stalin. He'd kill every last one of those stinking whites if he had the chance. I take a deep breath. Okay, okay. Two more weeks will tell the tale.

Well, two weeks later I'm back to 44,000. That's eleven thousand in two short weeks. Not only didn't the rituximab work, it seems to have kicked this blood cancer into overdrive. In September it was multiplying at 1000 a week. Now it's five times that. Is that what I get for going to war with my cancer, for being proactive? Is that a karmic butt kick or what?

During my next visit, the WBC is in the mid-fifties. I ask Dr. T, "What do we do now?"

"I'll prescribe some CVP," he says.

Bonnie seems to know what he's talking about. "CVP," she repeats.

I look at her, shrugging, palms up.

"It's a combination of chemotherapy drugs: cyclophosphamide, vincristine and prednisolone, which is a steroid," Dr. T says.

This is no help to me. The only one I know anything about is prednisolone or prednisone, the steroid. My mother, who had rheumatoid arthritis for sixty years, used it on a regular basis. It made her crazy, but she didn't know and/or didn't care. The other stuff, I learn, can make you sick and can be useful if you are interested in a full-body depilatory.

* * *

BONNIE:

Fortunately, Barry experiences no bad side effects from his Rituxan experiment. Unfortunately, after an initial lowering following the first treatment, the Rituxan has no effect at all. On the contrary, Barry's white blood count continues to skyrocket. By mid-April, it is up to 78,000. Barry is freaking out and so am I. To make matters even worse, Dr. T. comes up with yet another diagnosis—follicular lymphoma—and another chemo regimen for Barry to try, which also proves to be totally ineffective.

* * *

BARRY:

I discover that most of the time, oncologists prescribe CVP for use in conjunction with rituximab. This makes me skeptical. If rituximab didn't do anything but help my cancerous white blood cells put pedal to the metal, why would something that is often used in combination with rituximab do anything good for me? But I say nothing. I have to hope.

In April, I have my first infusion of CVP. My white blood count is now sixty-something. I've stopped counting the thousands now, just as with children there comes a point when you cease to use months to describe their age, moving on to only years.

A few days later, I go to a movie with my friend Jonah. We get to the theater early. They are cleaning and sweeping up, from the preceding show. There are people hanging around outside but no line at the door to get in. Jonah and I stand at the door. Finally, it opens. We start inside. Just then, a couple of supersized women jump up from the seats nearby and push in front of us.

"What's that all about?" I ask.

"We were here ahead of you," one sneers. "We were waiting right over there."

"I don't see any line," I reply.

She says something snarky. I don't remember what.

"Go ahead," I say. "It's a good thing the theater's empty because you'll need a full row to squeeze your fat asses in."

They gasp.

There's a chivalrous fellow standing behind me. He's half my age but not very intimidating. "You should watch your mouth," he pipes up.

"You with those fat bitches?" I ask.

"You're looking for trouble," he tells me.

"I'm not going to get very much of it from you."

He takes a step toward me. "Come right on, motherfucker," I growl, using the kind of hand signals you see when someone is communicating from the driver's seat.

"You're crazy," he says as he backs off.

He's right; I am crazy. "That was the prednisone talking," I whisper to Jonah as we take our seats in the sparsely populated theater. "I would have ripped his fucking head off. I'm really pumped."

Jonah nods, but I can see he's embarrassed.

I'm not all that concerned about getting hurt or even dying, really. It's the beginning of what a shrink might call my suicidal ideation. I'm too fucked up on that CVP shit to give a damn.

* * *

Bonnie and I trudge back in to see Dr. T for an April appointment. I am without any expectations. I don't think CVP is working, although I have no data to prove it—until I get to Dr. T's office. My latest blood draw confirms my dark outlook. My WBC is now in the nineties. The disease is shucking off these treatments like a raging bull parting the crowds of runners at Pamplona. It looks like nothing is going to stop it. Dr. T takes a look at the reports. "Well, it's not behaving like a B-cell lymphoma," he explains. "And you have a clonal population of T cells. It's starting to look a lot like T-cell lymphoma."

"So what are the treatments for T-cell lymphoma?" one of us asks.

"We don't have a lot for that disease," he confesses. He seems glum. "And it is a very aggressive form of lymphoma. I think it's time for you to get another opinion from the doctor at Stanford."

I know that already. I've just gone from forty thousand to ninety thousand in a matter of less than two months. Dr. T is clearly out of remedies and doesn't have much of a clue what to do next. We leave Dr. T's office without a treatment plan once again.

BONNIE:

We were scared. During our next to last appointment with Dr. T, he told us that Barry had a "clonal population" of T cells and that he was giving him yet another diagnosis: T-CLL. We looked at each other. What's a "clonal population?" I asked. Dr. T explained that it meant that bad cells were producing more of the same.

The next week he changes the diagnosis once again to T-cell prolymphocytic leukemia (T-PLL) after telling us that Dr. Coutre at Stanford doesn't think that T-CLL exists. He is sending us down to consult with Dr. Coutre again. During that last visit, we watch as he swivels in his chair and goes online to a lay medical site to look something up.

I go back to the Internet, searching as we wait for the appointment with Dr. Coutre at Stanford. The information about T-cell lymphoma is slim and mostly anecdotal—none of it good. If left untreated the average life expectancy of a victim of T-cell lymphoma is about seven months. Barry was diagnosed in July 2005. It is now April 2006.That's already eight or nine months. But he's still asymptomatic, so a survival span of diagnosis to death is meaningless. Most people in his condition wouldn't even have a diagnosis yet. Still, at the rate this thing is taking off, he'll probably have symptoms within a few months.

* * *

BARRY:

The Internet doesn't have much about treatments for T-PLL except to describe the failed treatments of the dearly departed. Basically, the stuff medical science throws at T-cell lymphomas can prolong that seven-month prognosis to a couple of years, according to statistics. The stories though don't paint a rosy picture of those extra seventeen months. I'm thinking that there's no point and spend the rest of the week crying, depressed, and sometimes in denial. I'm a wreck.

* * *

BONNIE:

Barry and I have very different outlooks on life. I'm the eternal optimist— some might call me a Pollyanna—and Barry is the eternal pessimist. For him, the glass isn't merely half empty; he isn't even holding the damned glass. How this has played out during our marriage, and particularly in relation to cancer, has been challenging. I have found myself in the position of cheerleader to his doom and gloom, even when I don't feel like cheerleading.

An example of this is how we react to what the doctors say and how we read test results. Looking back now, the signs were there all along that this was an aggressive disease. What I took away from the doctor visits and the pathology reports was every glimmer of hope (and denial) and no acknowledgement of the serious findings (the chromosomal abnormalities) or opinions (a future transplant). Barry only heard the word "cancer" and then tuned out.

While cancer highlighted our differences in approaches and temperament, it also brought us together in a way that was almost magical. We had a "good marriage" all along, but there had been stormy periods and some issues that would never go away. Since we had gotten married very young—I was 20 and Barry was 23—we essentially grew up together. Although, on paper, we came from very similar backgrounds, in reality our family-of-origin situations were very different. I've always felt that no matter how much you reject unfavorable aspects of your upbringing, you do bring it along to your marriage and child raising. And we both did.

But these temperamental style differences were minor. I certainly did not appreciate some aspects of Barry's temper and he did not appreciate my inability to live with chaos. Fortunately, many major issues that can negatively impact a marriage were not there for us. We never fought about money. Infidelity only reared its ugly head once early on and was quickly resolved, and we honestly enjoyed each other's company. Most of our battles were about inconsequential things.

We enriched each other's lives. Before we met, I had never hiked or camped, or done anything very physical or outdoorsy. And Barry had not attended live theater performances. One of his dreams was to build a house in the country and we did that together—the actual building of it! It was not my dream, but it worked out. We traveled well together and had rituals like reading the paper and discussing the news together in the morning. We did that almost every morning of our lives. That's one of the things I would miss the most.

* * *

BARRY:

Bonnie is frantic. She's poring over Internet articles, trying her best to understand what she's reading. She's not giving up. Her tenacity encourages me to give it a try myself. Almost simultaneously we discover information about a new monoclonal antibody that was developed in England and has had some success treating T-cell lymphomas. It's called Campath and it appears to have just crossed the Atlantic for clinical trials. Clinical shminical. I'll go to England if I have to. I start rummaging through boxes of old documents. I am registered with the British National Health Service from when I was a student at the University of Manchester back in the mid-Sixties. Maybe they'll still accept me as a patient. And if not, I'm sure I can wangle something.

I call Dr. T and ask him whether he has ever heard of Campath. He hasn't. I give him the URLs for the articles we found. He says he'll take a look. Before he gets back to me though, I will have my second visit with Dr. Coutre at Stanford.

* * *

BONNIE:

Luckily, Barry gets an appointment quickly with Dr. Coutre. Taking his time with us, he explains, as well as he can to lay people, what is going on. Of course, nothing is completely clear, but his thought processes are transparent. This guy really knows his stuff, I think. We breathe a sigh of relief when he goes back to the original diagnosis, CLL, and suggests a brand new treatment—Campath—something that we had also encountered during our Internet surfing.

The drive back is MUCH better than the drive down. Once more we have hope there is a treatment and we feel like we've just received a reprieve from the frightening seven-month diagnosis. We look at each other and, reading each other's minds, simultaneously ask: "Why are we continuing with Dr. T? We should just get treated at Stanford, where they know their stuff."

I call from the car and tell Dr. Coutre's assistant we'd like Barry to be treated by him, and we are on our way.

Having a plan always soothes me, so instead of tears and fears for the future, I make lists (my way of coping) of people to contact, vacations to re-schedule, all the things that needed doing and all the things that really didn't matter. And I write my first email to family and friends. I have hope …

May 5, 2006
Update on Barry's Health

Dear Family & Friends,

As some of you know, last week Barry got a very dire interim diagnosis. Today we went to see Dr. Coutre at Stanford who told us the following good news:

1. Barry does NOT have a T-cell lymphoma. He has a clonal population of T cells and may have had them all along. They might develop into a T-cell lymphoma, or not.

2. He is sticking with the CLL (chronic lymphocytic leukemia) diagnosis, as well as possibly another B-cell lymphoma.

3. Neither the Rituxan nor the chemo (CVP) has done anything to ameliorate the disease condition, as Barry's white blood count and lymphocyte count are still rising fast. Barry has a chromosomal abnormality that precludes these two treatments from working.

4. Barry is still asymptomatic, his lymph nodes are not enlarged, and his spleen (where he has been experiencing pain) is not terribly enlarged.

5. He will start on Campath, another monoclonal antibody, which is better at treating bone marrow and peripheral blood as opposed to lymph nodes.

We liked Dr. Coutre very much and are switching to him as Barry's primary oncologist. He described Barry as "young," which we particularly liked.

As the Campath is a twelve to eighteen week treatment regimen with no terrible side effects other than a compromised immune system susceptible to viral infections, we will most likely be postponing or canceling most of our summer travel.

We will also be looking into stem cell/bone marrow transplant with a specialist at Stanford who has been doing a lot of work on CLL transplants. While there is presently no cure for CLL, they have been having good success treating it with Campath, and possibly curing it with the transplant.

We both thank you all so, so much for your love and support. It's now been nine months since Barry got the first diagnosis of CLL from our primary care doc. I don't think we could have traveled this miserable path without all of you. And we're still marching along . . .

With love and hope,
Bonnie

* * *

BARRY:

A few days after Bonnie sent that email I get a phone call at home from Dr. T. "I've looked into Campath," he says. "I think it may be a good treatment option for you."

"We know," I tell him, assuming that Dr. Coutre has forwarded his report to him. "Dr. Coutre has recommended that I begin a course of Campath treatment. We've decided to do the treatment at Stanford."

"I can arrange for you to get the shots up here in our offices," he says.

Last week he didn't have a clue what Campath was. This week he says he is competent to administer this treatment. From the time he started me on Rituxan less than four months ago, my WBC tripled. He didn't have a clue that I have an abnormality that would prevent either of the two treatments he prescribed from working. Dr. Coutre knew it right away. I have to take a deep breath. There's a possibility he is trying to help, although what I'm really thinking is that Campath runs about eleven grand a shot and I'm scheduled for at least thirty-six of them. Plus, he wouldn't know a complication if it smacked him in the face. On the motive scale, benign is low, self-interest is extremely high, and concern for my wellbeing is not on the chart. I can't say I'm not bitter that Dr. T, who knew or should have known he was in way over his head, didn't hand me off to a specialist sooner. His waiting room is full. His infusion chairs always have a butt in them. He's got enough business as it is. Why does he want to keep me as a patient when he knows Stanford has experience administering this new drug, and he has none?

For a moment, I have this twinge of discomfort. I don't want to hurt his feelings. But there comes a point when you've just got to make a decision. It's either wounding your doctor's ego or your own health. I get a grip. It's my life we're talking about here, but all he seems to be concerned about is cutting himself in on the Campath profits. "Thanks, Dr. T," I reply, "but we've decided to change treating physicians. Dr. Coutre has said he's willing to take me on, and he has experience with Campath. Thanks for all your help." Click.

BONNIE:

What a summer! We must cancel four trips, including Barry's fortieth college reunion where he was scheduled to read from a novel he'd written, and also my family reunion. These cancellations are extremely difficult for me as I live for vacations. We settle into a routine of driving to Stanford, Barry getting a shot in the abdomen, meeting with Coutre and counting the weeks. We learn that the "Cam" in Campath stands for Cambridge University in England where it was developed. The U.S. trials were conducted at Stanford, and several of our favorite nurses were actually reps and very familiar with the drug. They are reassuring and we feel cared for. In fact, we are befriended by many of the nurses in the ITA (Infusion Treatment Area) BMT (Blood and Marrow Transplant)/Hematology Unit), and were it not for our purpose in being there, it might have seemed like a social occasion.

Then, just when we thought that we were on a roll, Blue Shield denied coverage for the Campath. They said that Barry should have been treated with Fludarabine. At $11,000 a shot, Campath would have cost us around $400,000. Yikes! Barry was freaked, but I was pretty calm about it. I was confident that Stanford was doing the right thing and that we were not going to have to pay $400,000. When we talked with Dr. Coutre about this turn of events, perhaps hysterically, he shook his head. He said that they should know that with Barry's chromosomal abnormalities, and a diagnosis of an aggressive form of CLL, not the indolent kind, Fludarabine would not work, would cost money, and would delay a successful treatment option so that they would end up paying for it anyway. Dr. Coutre took over dealing with Blue Shield. He faxed them articles from peer-reviewed medical journals, wrote them letters and finally, after several months, convinced them to cover the treatment. We don't really know what they ended up paying, but I'm sure it was way less than $400,000. We breathed sighs of relief.

This ability to convince an insurance company to do the right thing was an unanticipated benefit of being at a teaching hospital where they know way more than the insurance people. The insurance protocol might have deprived Barry of an opportunity for a transplant. Once again we struck gold in the luck department.

CHAPTER FOUR

The Hero's Cure

BONNIE:

July 1, 2006
Latest on Barry's Health

Dear Family & Friends,
    Things are looking good. Barry has completed two-thirds of his Campath treatment and his blood work has been normal since week three. We drive down to Stanford three times a week for a shot in his abdomen. He gets blood taken every Monday and we see the doctor every two weeks. The doctor is very pleased with the results and told us Barry is having "the best possible response." When the treatment ends on July 28, we have a week off, then we will go to our yoga retreat in Montana (great timing!) and Barry will have a bone marrow biopsy when we return. It doesn't matter if his blood work is normal—what matters is whether the marrow has been affected by the treatment.
    The side effects of the treatment for Barry have been extreme fatigue (many naps) and two infections, both expected, and both treatable. We have been trying to lead a quiet life during this twelve-week, seemingly unending, treatment period. We are watching a lot of comedy and movies, eating simply, going to our wonderful Saturday yoga class and both keeping up with our work lives as much as possible. We will meet with Dr. David Miklos, the bone marrow transplant doctor, in two weeks to start exploring that option, if it becomes necessary.
    Thanks again for all of your love and support. It means the world.
    With love and hope,
    Bonnie

* * *

BARRY:

"I'm a car salesman," Dr. David Miklos says. We are in one of those ubiquitous Stanford Cancer Center treatment rooms—windowless, spanking clean with a computer able to call up all my records. It is July 15, 2006 and I'm nearly done with the Campath treatment. My blood tests show that my WBC is well within normal range. I'm breathing easier. Bonnie and I are thinking there's a possibility that I'm cured.

This is just an informational interview. I'm hoping that maybe I won't need a transplant. Maybe Campath has done the trick. I'll listen politely but I'm not in the market for a car, or a new brand of blood. I don't like salesmen—car salesmen especially—so he's chosen the wrong metaphor for my sensibilities.

Dr. Miklos is a young doctor—at least from my point of view. He is clean cut, neat and has a wry smile. "You're in remission at the moment," he says. "This is the absolute best time for a stem-cell transplant."

"But maybe the Campath has worked," I suggest hesitantly. "Maybe I don't need a transplant."

Dr. Miklos shakes his head. "Campath gets you into remission. It doesn't keep you there. Sooner or later the CLL will come back, and when it does Campath won't work as well the second time. The only way to get cured is to have a transplant."

Bonnie has been researching transplants. "Isn't a transplant dangerous? I've heard that they are high-risk."

Dr. Miklos is pulling no punches. "Right now about five percent of those receiving a transplant die during the first few months. A transplant used to require that we wipe out your immune system, but we've gotten better at it. Now it's not a total ablative procedure, so the risk is lower, but yes, there is a significant risk of death. And after the treatment is over there is also a risk of GVHD, graft versus host disease. That is where your body tries to reject the graft. GVHD can cause lots of bad side effects that can be chronic—for the rest of your life—and GVHD can also kill you. But it's the only route we presently have to a complete cure. If it works, you will have an entirely new blood system."

I look at Bonnie with a long face. I thought that the Campath could be a cure; now I'm being told that the automotive repair is only a stopgap measure. I may get a few thousand miles more out of the old machine but I'm going to need a new engine pretty soon.

"We don't usually like to perform a transplant on people over sixty or who have other medical complications," Dr. Miklos continues, "but you're just sixty-one and appear to be in very good shape. Your chart seems to indicate that you are capable of withstanding the difficulties of a transplant."

Over the many years of my legal career, I have become an expert in detecting and litigating fraud. One of the hallmarks of a fraudulent pitch is urgency. The victim is told that the offer is about to expire and that they have to make their decision fast. That's what I just heard. Yikes!

"And sometimes it takes a long time to find a compatible donor," Dr. Miklos adds. "Sometimes we never find a donor. We have trouble especially with people of mixed race, Europeans, and strangely, Pacific Islanders."

Well at least I'm not that. I'm an Ashkenazi Jew on both sides. And we're a pretty small group, not known until recently for a whole lot of intermarriage. We're all sort of cousins. At least I've got that going for me. It never occurred to me that this self-selecting ingrown population would have any benefits. Usually we get "chosen" to be the scapegoat when something turns to shit and a leader/dictator has to resort to demagoguery to stay in power. Besides, every synagogue worth its kosher salt has had a leukemia donor drive at some point in the past few years. So chances are the donor bank has someone who can be a match. I can feel myself buying in.

"We might as well get that ball rolling now," Dr. Miklos suggests. "It could take a while to find somebody who is suitable, and you don't have to make a decision right away." He then launches into an explanation of the transplant process. The big words are flying. The references to the other transplant centers, Hutchinson, M.D. Anderson, Mayo Clinic, Johns Hopkins, their success and failure statistics go in one ear and out the other. Bonnie takes notes. I do my usual tune-out thing. What I retain is that five percent die right off the bat, and of those who make it through, a bunch get GVHD and some of them croak. Another group ends up having to take steroids for the rest of their lives, making me recall my trip to the movies with Jonah. Does getting shot by an irate adversary count in the statistics?

After the meeting we are cruising along Interstate 280, heading north to home. To our left the pristine watershed for San Francisco—long thin lakes of shimmering turquoise fill the valley created by the San Andreas Fault. Beyond the lakes a ridgeline of evergreens cuts a saw blade horizon into the clear blue summer sky. I want to live to see more of these afternoons, more such scenery that, until recently, I have taken for granted. "I thought that the Campath would do it," I say solemnly to Bonnie.

"Me too," she says. "You know, if you do the transplant, we'll have to move to Palo Alto to be near the treatment center. I'll have to take a leave from my job. They say that patients need a caregiver twenty-four/seven. It will change our lives even more than it has already."

During the rest of the trip home, we're lost in thought, imagining how our lives are going to be different, perhaps permanently. And I might not make it. How long will I be okay with just the Campath, I ask myself. And what if a transplant does not cure me? What if I have two years now, the way I am? What if I get a transplant next month and die? I've just tossed away two years. I repeat these thoughts aloud.

"What if we get hit by a truck in ten minutes?" Bonnie replies.

* * *

BONNIE:

The first time we met him we did not like David Miklos, the transplant doc. We had just endured a long wait and were a little miffed to begin with, and when he walked into the room he seemed like a glad-hander. Just about the first thing he did was describe himself as a used car salesman, and he sounded exactly like one, exuding bravado that was off-putting. His pitch was full of extremely complex and technical scientific language.

Do we even want a stem cell transplant from this guy? I wondered. The Campath is working just fine. Won't the Campath just keep the CLL at bay? But when we raised that issue he dashed our hopes.

"It may work for a time, but Barry's aggressive CLL will likely return within about six months," he said, "and Campath can't be counted on to work a second time. It's done its job preparing Barry for a transplant by cleaning out the cancer cells. There's only one cure for CLL: a transplant. I call it the hero's cure. It has the upfront risk of death during the treatment, but if it works, you get the long-term benefit."

He explained the transplant process in scary detail. Although it's called a transplant, it's really an infusion of adult stem cells. It is not a surgical procedure and, unlike solid organ transplants, does not require lifelong anti-rejection medication.

The kind of transplant Barry would be receiving is called a non-myeloablative allogeneic stem cell transplant. The "non-myeloablative" part refers to the pre-treatment, the partial, as opposed to the complete (myeloablative) killing of Barry's immune system. Allogeneic means from a donor, as opposed to one's own treated stem cells. He said that, instead of total body irradiation, Barry will receive total lymphoid irradiation (TLI); and instead of heavy-duty chemotherapy, they'll use ATG, a milder monoclonal antibody derived from rabbits (!!!). This regimen, developed at Stanford, has been very successful in preventing acute graft versus host disease (GVHD), which can be lethal.

The cells will have to come from an unrelated donor, as Barry has no potential family donors. (It turns out that men have better outcomes with female donors. Who knew?)

A stem cell transplant is basically an outpatient process. If it happens, we'll have to move down to Palo Alto for about four months. Barry will have to spend five days in the hospital being treated with ATG first, then after an additional week of radiation, he'll receive the donor cells in a physical blood transfusion. Risks involved GVHD, both acute and chronic as well as a return of the cancer.

Still, Dr. Miklos was reassuring. He described Stanford's protocol as a kinder, gentler graft. He gave us some sparse but positive statistics, warning that if we didn't move quickly it might be too late. Sometimes it takes a long time to locate a donor. Some people die waiting. Barry was not happy to hear any of this, but agreed to do the testing to find a donor. This shocked me because I was still in denial that it was necessary.

"What about health insurance?" I ask Dr. Miklos. I have spent many hours dealing with these miscreants, fighting with them, filling out their damn forms, and faxing paperwork they claim to have never received.

"The BMT unit at Stanford has two full-time people who deal with the insurance companies," he assured us. "You won't have to do anything related to that aspect of transplant."

I was relieved, and it turned out to be completely true.

When we'd walked in for our appointment, we naively thought that Dr. Miklos was going to ask us why we were even there, since Campath had been so successful. Instead we were now looking at making quick decisions that could lead to death in a matter of months, or horrible life-long side-effects. We walked out of this two-hour appointment sobered by the immediacy of the risks and the statistics, Dr. Miklos's reassurances notwithstanding.

Maybe Coutre would disagree? We hoped so and were anxious to talk to him again. But when we met with him about ten days later our hopes were dashed. He agreed with Dr. Miklos that a transplant was the only potential cure. Turning on my tape recorder, I asked him what Barry's prognosis would be if we stuck with Campath. "Barry will die," he said.

During that ten-day interim, we got more used to the idea of a transplant. It had been a year since diagnosis and the rollercoaster of emotions was not letting up—despair, disbelief, hope, denial, excitement and terror. We were now convinced that the transplant was necessary.

* * *

BONNIE:

July 25, 2006
Bone Marrow/Stem Cell Transplant

Dear Family & Friends,
Today marks exactly one year from Barry's diagnosis of CLL during a routine physical.

Ten days ago we met with a bone marrow transplant doctor at Stanford, Dr. Miklos, who recommended a transplant as early as mid-September. After spending time recovering from this shock and exploring his reasons, which made sense, we met with Dr. Coutre, Barry's regular hematologist. While we thought (hoped) that Campath, the treatment Barry has been receiving for the last twelve weeks, could possibly be a cure, we have learned that the only potential cure is the transplant. Because of Barry's clonal population of T cells as well as his chromosomal abnormalities, he has an aggressive form of CLL that will definitely re-occur and likely lead to death. Both of these doctors are CLL specialists and top-notch research docs. We feel like we are in good hands.

We have not scheduled the transplant, but it will most likely occur sometime between November and March. While this is not emergency surgery, we have been told that Barry will have a better outcome the sooner he does it. We do not yet know whether the Campath has cleared Barry's bone marrow. That biopsy will not happen until late August, a month after treatment ends.

We have started the ball rolling on identifying a donor through the National Marrow Donor Program. This could take some time, and if a donor is not found, we will conduct a drive among family and friends (that would be all of you). The transplant itself is done mostly outpatient and we will move to Palo Alto for four months. The entire process, including recovery, will take about a year.

We just spent a wonderful weekend in Carmel and will be going to the Feathered Pipe Ranch in Montana for our yoga retreat August 5–12. We

plan on a couple of more vacations and trips before the transplant.
Barry is doing very well emotionally and is feeling very hopeful. He has
become the Zen master of life.
Lots of love,
Bonnie

*   *   *

BARRY:

I have my friend Stan Goldberg to thank for that "Zen master of life" thing. Stan is a fellow member of the Blackpoint Writers' Group. We share driving duties to its meetings every Thursday evening, and we talk a lot about health on the trips up and back. Stan has prostate cancer and it's way more serious than the one I had. He's writing about how his experience with cancer led him to volunteer at a local hospice and the enlightenment he received by working with dying patients. His stories are poignant and he's a wonderful writer so he is able to tap into his readers' emotions.

On one trip, I asked Stan whether he'd noticed any common threads between those who experience a peaceful death and those who have a troubled and difficult passing. (It'd been just a few years since my mother died. I was at her bedside for most of her final week. She had a hard time of it.) I was very curious to learn his observations.

Stan nodded. Indeed, he had some insights on this topic. "People who have unfinished business have a hard time dying," he said. "If there is someone whom they've hurt and failed to reconcile with, failed to apologize to, then they experience a lot of anguish and regret in their last days. Death comes to them hard. People who have settled their accounts have an easier time."

Stan's observations were an explanation for what I'd seen first-hand during my mother's death process. On the third morning before she passed away, she woke, looked around and said: "Oh, I'm still here. I can't even die right." There weren't a lot of things that I agreed with my mother on, but that comment was the truth. Her final days peeled back layer after layer of phony rationalizations to reveal a tormented soul. She was scrolling through her memories, reliving every resentment, torturously justifying every wrong she'd ever done. She accused her sister-in-law of hating her and conspiring to alienate her brother's affections. She made derogatory racial comments about her underpaid (and under-appreciated) caregivers.

When my father sat crying at her bedside and blubbered: "We had a wonderful life together," she scowled and ordered him to leave the room. She lied to me, concealing that in her last two weeks, she'd seen a lawyer to change her estate plan to cut me out, all the while pretending that we were on perfectly fine terms. Her last moments were wasted in anguished rationalizations that made me squirm with discomfort.

I didn't wait for the end. After four days of it, I'd had enough. She'd left matters just the way she'd sowed them, a bitter harvest, and she paid the price. I had to take care of my own business now, and I didn't want that for me. So I guess that turned into something Zen, and I think I became the better for it.

* * *

BONNIE:

August 12, 2006
Trip to Stanford Hospital Instead of Montana

Dear Ones,

Barry ended up in the hospital last week with a serious infection (listeriosis), which led to early sepsis, a blood infection. His fever got as high as 105 and then dropped precipitously, as did his blood pressure. He was very seriously ill and we are very grateful to the Stanford docs/nurses for saving his life. Unpasteurized mozzarella cheese was the culprit, and now he is on a somewhat restricted diet until he gets a new immune system, hopefully this fall.

He is home now with a PICC line inserted and getting IV Ampicillin for about another week. He will be cured of this infection, but it was a wake-up call as to his disease state.

Love,
Bonnie

* * *

BARRY:

On August 2, one of those "duh" moments nearly killed me. Dinner that evening was one of my summertime favorites: heirloom tomatoes, mozzarella and basil on sweet French bread. I was a novice when it came to compromised immune systems and hadn't a clue how effective Campath was at giving me one. No one was paying attention to this side effect, even though I'd had two minor infections already. No one warned me about the risks of consuming unpasteurized cheese. (Pregnant women also are at high risk.)

After dinner we went to a friend's house. I was feeling a little shaky and tired but that was not extraordinary, given the side effects I'd been experiencing after three months of Campath. I felt woozy on the walk home and went to bed early. Around three a.m. I awoke freezing cold. It was not a particularly chilly night, even by summertime San Francisco standards. I put on pajamas but couldn't stop shivering. Bonnie and I decided that we should give it a couple hours and see how it went.

At six, I was still freezing but now it was alternating with fevers. My extremities were shaking, and thinking clearly was out of the question. Bonnie called Stanford Cancer Center and was told to bring me right in. On the way, I should drink as much liquids as possible.

We filled a thermos with OJ and set out for Stanford in the early morning alongside the Porsches and BMWs of the high tech commuters. I drank the juice and promptly threw it up. When we got to the Infusion Treatment Area they put me in a treatment room and began packing me with ice. I was clearly a priority.

The next thing I recall, I was on a gurney and watching ceiling tiles pass by as I was pushed out of the ITA and into the regular hospital. Things were pretty hazy. I remember Bonnie asking about antibiotics. I'd been given some antibiotics or antivirals for both for my previous two infections and they had put me right within a couple of days. She seemed to expect the same.

It was Wednesday. We had plane tickets for Montana for Saturday, our eagerly awaited yoga retreat. She wanted reassurance that we'd be out of the hospital in a day or two and could be on our way, but wasn't getting it.

Every year for more than a decade, Bonnie attended a yoga retreat at the Feathered Pipe Ranch outside of Helena, Montana. For about seven of those years, I accompanied her. We had friends in Helena that we visited on the same trip. There were people we looked forward to spending the week with every year. And the yoga was a welcome respite from our daily lives of stress. We were heading into the most stressful experience of our lives. This year, more than ever before, Bonnie needed the comfort of a week away, doing nothing but yoga and relaxation.

So as I lay on my hospital bed, hopped up on antibiotics, antivirals, and whatever else they were pushing into my system, I'd look over to see

Bonnie's complexion growing increasingly drawn as the minutes and hours ticked off. I knew that part of it was anxiety—first that we wouldn't have much time to pack, but later that we wouldn't be going at all. She began to weep. I began to feel guilty. This was all my fault.

By Friday, it was clear that we wouldn't be making our Saturday flight. Bonnie spent some of the time arranging for a flight on Tuesday. Perhaps we could salvage most of the week. Perhaps we could salvage something.

As Sunday rolled around, it became obvious her hopes for a yoga retreat had been a will-o-the-wisp. We weren't going anywhere. It was around that point that the message was gently conveyed—I had been close to death. That delay we'd decided upon at three in the morning (to give it a few hours) nearly killed me. It was probably during those hours that sepsis had set in.

Sepsis happens when the body is fighting off a severe infection that has spread via the bloodstream. People who have a compromised immune system are frequent victims of sepsis. If it gets bad, your blood pressure will drop, as did mine. You will go into shock and if untreated or belatedly treated, you die. Three months of Campath had compromised my immune system. I was high risk for sepsis, but it never showed up on my radar. In retrospect, I should have been warned about things like non-pasteurized cheese, but if anybody had mentioned it, it never registered.

That summer, Bonnie and I were in la la land. The Campath had cured me. There were no residual downsides. I could eat anything. Do anything. Go anywhere. We wanted so much to be living our old (healthy) lives that, wherever possible, we made assumptions that accommodated that lifestyle. It was natural. It was understandable and proved, almost, to be lethal.

That experience, more than anything else, convinced me that I was going to go for the stem cell transplant. Two weeks before, on that trip home up I-280, I'd been delusional. I was weighing a phantasmagorical two-year life expectancy against a possible quick death during the transplant procedure. Then, I'd almost been run over by that truck.

* * *

BONNIE:

We were so looking forward to our annual trip to the Feathered Pipe Ranch just outside of Helena, Montana for a week of yoga with Judith

Hanson Lasater and our many "yoga friends." Barry had his last Campath treatment Friday, July 28, and we were preparing to fly out on Saturday, August 5. The timing was perfect, especially since we'd had to cancel or re-schedule every other trip that summer.

On Wednesday night we walked to our Book Club and had a great discussion. About 2:00 a.m. Barry woke up with serious chills. Since it was the middle of the night, and we did not want our sleep disturbed, we decided to wait until morning to see if he improved. About 6:00 he was worse and we took his temperature. It was 104! We called Stanford and they said to come in right away and that he would most likely be admitted. (Of course I did not believe that.) The nurse also told us to keep him hydrated so I put some orange juice, Barry's favorite, in a thermos and we got on the road.

The scene in the ITA was chaotic. The OJ did not agree with Barry, so I held a barf pan for him. One nurse was taking blood from one arm while another was putting an IV in the other. He was very sick with a raging infection. I called work and told them I wouldn't be in that day. After a short time, he was admitted to an isolation room with a beautiful garden right outside the window.

While waiting for the blood cultures to come back, Barry was being pumped full of broad-spectrum antibiotics. They told us the cultures wouldn't be back until Saturday. Clueless, I said, "That's too late because we're going to Montana on Saturday."

That first night was a bad one. I was able to stay in Barry's room on a cot, which was great, but also scary. During the night, both his temperature and his blood pressure dropped precipitously. The doctors and nurses were in and out and I just lay there in fear. I was aware that they were very concerned but what could I do? I just needed to stay out of their way and let them work on him. It was early sepsis. He almost died.

During those first couple of days I was still planning on flying to Montana. The doctors and nurses kept telling me that we weren't going to be able to go, but I would hear none of it. It wasn't until Friday afternoon that I KIND of got it and re-scheduled our flight for Tuesday. On Saturday the cultures came back and showed listeriosis. Barry was going to be at Stanford for a few more days and I finally canceled our trip.

A few days later I received this email from a dear yoga friend:

Dear Bonnie and Barry,
I just wanted you to know how much you two are missed this week.

Each time we come out of the teacher's cabin and look across at the Honeymoon Cabin, your home away from home, we send our love to you in San Francisco.

When we found out you weren't able to come this year, two women were moved from a yurt into the Honeymoon Cabin, and Judith made very clear that they could stay there this year, but that it was reserved for you two as always for next summer.

You two dears have many friends here and we send our love and prayers for your well-being across the skies.

With warm wishes and love,

Geri Herbert

Our friends were thinking about next year. Were we?

When we came home on Tuesday Barry had a PICC line for antibiotics that were delivered to the house. I searched the refrigerator and found the listeria-carrying culprit, unpasteurized mozzarella cheese.

We hadn't realized that the Campath had compromised Barry's immune system so that an opportunistic infection could come in and almost kill him. Unfortunately, the Stanford docs hadn't realized that either and he had not been on a restricted diet. Now he was, and would be for over a year. CLL was the real deal. Denial time was over. Any doubts about the need for a transplant were shattered.

CHAPTER FIVE

Jumping Hurdles to a Transplant

BARRY:

I dislike war metaphors when it comes to my relationship with cancer but I don't feel the same way about cancer treatment. I think of cancer treatment as a quintessential form of warfare. Our doctors are primed to fight it. Western medicine uses treatments that involve swords (surgery), fire (radiation) and weapons of mass destruction (chemo). To me, the interesting thing about stem cell transplants is that, except for the preparation, the concept involves something other than a frontal assault. A stem cell transplant involves an infusion of someone else's blood. It's sort of like infiltration—a fifth column inserted into the cellular population to alter the composition of the blood.

I like to think of a stem cell transplant as similar to *The Invasion of the Body Snatchers*—the allegory about our nice, comfy, complacent '50s society getting subverted by evil, mindless robotic life forms. (Some read communists while others interpret it as an anti-McCarthy screed.) In the original version, before the studio executives got cold feet—that the movie-going public would freak—and made the producers add a prologue and epilogue, the body snatchers actually take over and change civilization. Today, we'd demand the opportunity to debate the issue. At least we've come that far.

Anyway, I've opted for the body snatchers. I don't want to spend the rest of what looks to be an abbreviated life waiting for another frigid wake up call at three a.m., another panic-stricken wild ride to the hospital and an inevitable fadeout. I've looked death in the face once now and I'm ready to do it again. It's put up or shut up time. I don't like it, but it feels like what I imagine it must for a soldier on the eve of battle. You've just chalked yourself up as a casualty and you've now become a member of the ghoul army.

The lead-up to a transplant is intense. Mine came with a speed that I hadn't anticipated. They found a donor within two weeks. In fact, they came up with five acceptable matches and Dr. Miklos had the luxury of picking the one he most preferred. It was a feast of good fortune, an auspicious beginning.

Dr. Miklos selected a female donor because he wanted there to be some conflict between the donated cells and my own. How had he guessed I was likely to have gender conflicts? (I have three daughters and no sons.) Was there something more symbolic going on here?

Monday morning, Sept. 18, 2006, I had the second of my many bone marrow biopsies and it was a doozy. They set me up with some inexperienced fellow who had the skillful touch of a jackhammer operator and the empathy of a concentration camp guard. If you've never had a bone marrow biopsy, my recommendation is to avoid it. If you can't avoid it, demand every type of painkiller available. Ask to be knocked out. What they do is take a hollow needle—a needle big and strong enough to inject a horse—and jamb it into your pelvis. They have to push it through the bone and into the marrow. Once it gets there they suck out a bunch of marrow and it feels just like you'd imagine if someone was using a straw to suck up the ice cream at the bottom of a milkshake, except that it's your marrow that's the ice cream. You feel it getting pulled out of your bones even when you've been sedated. And after they've drunk their fill of your marrow, they're not quite done. They have to snip off a piece of your bone so they can take a peek at that too. I've had fourteen of them as of this writing. I've had them done by the good, the bad, and the ugly. This, my second BMB, was done by the bad and ugly.

In the afternoon I had a PET scan. This involved an injection of radioactive dye and a stretch on my back inside a tube, where I couldn't move for about forty minutes. Of course, it was during those forty minutes that my nose began to itch like crazy.

With my donor identified they scheduled my hospitalization for late October. I was giving away all of my remaining cases, shucking my lawyer identity. Bonnie was beginning to lay the groundwork for a lengthy leave of absence from work and new assignments as my full-time caregiver. Our cozy home life was turned upside down. We needed to shop for a temporary, fully-furnished apartment near Stanford. We needed to make arrangements for our kids to hold down the old homestead in our absence. There were lists of things that we needed to bring, and other things we had to cancel. Lots of people needed to be notified. Everything was swirling and we were scared. We'd look at each other and ask: "Is life as we've known it really over? Is this how it ends?"

Two days later, Bonnie and I went to therapy with Rodney Shapiro. We needed it. The day of reckoning was rapidly approaching. It wasn't like we were dealing with a sudden death or even the certainty of a terminal illness. We were about to embark into a perilous unknown and that made our emotions erratic. At times like that, a therapist comes in handy.

The next day, I got a haircut from Carolyn. I'd been going to her for close to twenty years. I didn't know whether I'd ever get another haircut from her, or anyone else, so we said a goodbye as if it was the last time. I had Stan in mind. This is the way to do it, I told myself.

* * *

BONNIE:

We had our last meeting with Dr. Coutre. He once again emphasized the urgency of the transplant and cautioned us that if Barry's disease came back, the transplant would not work. So we moved forward with preparations for the transplant—convinced it would happen even though many hurdles needed to be overcome. Barry needed to pass a multitude of tests to ensure that he was a good candidate. He was now under the care of Dr. Miklos. It was kind of strange, as we never saw Dr. Coutre again during the transplant process, except in passing.

During this time we also had our first meeting with a social worker at Stanford. She helped us with housing information and gave Barry information about applying for Social Security disability. She also told me about the caregiver classes given at Stanford that I could attend. She impressed upon us the crucial role of the caregiver and gave us a 217-page binder entitled "Allogeneic Blood and Marrow Transplant Guidebook" that I still refer to. Here's a sampling:

> "Blood and marrow transplantation is an aggressive therapy used to treat a variety of diseases. ... Transplantation is a difficult experience both physically and emotionally. ... You will need to have a family member or friend act as your bone marrow transplant caregiver for one to four months during the outpatient portion of your transplant. ...

"The responsibilities of the ... caregiver include:

- *Grocery shopping and meal preparation*
- *Supervision of fluid intake*
- *Recording food and fluid intake*
- *Boiling water when patients are at risk of infections*
- *Monitoring medication and filling prescriptions*
- *Housekeeping and laundry*
- *Assistance with central venous catheter and IV infusion pumps*
- *Keeping track of patient's symptoms*
- *Transportation*
- *Gatekeeping to insure patient gets adequate rest*
- *Communications with friends and family*
- *Companionship*
- *Emotional support*
- *Spiritual support."*

Caregivers are warned that these tasks are a full-time responsibility and that the job is stressful. The Guidebook goes on to say: "Several research studies have shown that family members are affected by all stages of the transplant process and may find themselves exhausted, stressed, and anxious." This, I came to discover, to put it mildly.

It was time to arrange to be away from work for four months. Fortunately, I had a great job. My employer and all of my co-workers were completely supportive. Even though the company I worked for, Simpson, Gumpertz, and Heger, was required by law to grant me Family Medical Leave, they weren't required by law to be nice about it. But they were more than nice. My co-workers pitched in to make sure that my leave would be smooth and that I would not have to worry about anything.

On September 18, Barry had a bone marrow biopsy. The first biopsy, done by Dr. T, had been a breeze because Barry was given Versed. Stanford does not use Versed. (We have asked many times why this is so, but have never been given a satisfactory response.) The Hematology fellow who did Barry's biopsy on that day was horrible. Barry has a very high threshold of pain and he was screaming. The pain was excruciating and she just kept going. "It will just be a little longer," she said, instead of backing off. He was traumatized. Fortunately, we got a call a few days later saying that the results were as good as they could be. No leukemia. We were on our way.

Sept. 21, 2006
The Transplant Is On

Dear Family and Friends,
As some of you know, Barry had a bone marrow biopsy on Monday to see whether the treatment he went through this summer (Campath, a monoclonal antibody) had cleared his marrow enough to make him a viable candidate for a bone marrow/stem cell transplant. We got a call today from the doctor's office at Stanford with great news—there is no sign of leukemia in his marrow.
Things have been moving fast on the transplant front. A well-matched donor has been identified through the National Marrow Donor Program and we have a full calendar of appointments, tests, trainings, and procedures ending with a pre-transplant one-week hospitalization on October 22 and the transplant scheduled for November 3. We will be moving to an apartment across the street from the hospital the week of October 22, and will stay there up to four months. We are very optimistic that Barry will be cured of his CLL (chronic lymphocytic leukemia) and by next year some time our life will resume a more normal pattern. For those of you interested, check out http://bmt.stanford.edu/ where Barry is being treated. He will be having a non-myeloablative allogeneic BMT. Non-myeloablative means that they will try not to destroy Barry's entire immune system but just suppress it so the transplant will take. Allogeneic means that the cells they will use for the transplant come from a donor and will not be Barry's own cells cleaned up. For those of you who are interested in getting in the donor bank, check out http://marrow.org/.
Please forgive me if I don't return emails and phone calls. We've been trying to live a quiet life, and also watch a lot of comedy. We want to wish all of you and the world a peaceful, healthy and sweet New Year.
Much love,
Bonnie

* * *

BARRY:

The following Monday I had a pulmonary function test to make sure that my heart would be up to whatever crap they were going to put me through. I had a short meeting with virology, just so they'd be familiar with my history. Little did I know how much I'd need that department, or how soon. In the afternoon, they had me penciled in for an echocardiogram, and after that a meeting at dermatology. These stem cell transplants are known to cause all sorts of skin rashes, and worse.

* * *

BONNIE:

Now we entered a whirlwind of activity. We rented a furnished apartment right across the street from the hospital and started to make plans for our move. The apartment was tiny, compared to our big house—one bedroom, one bath and a cramped kitchen, but that was fine with me. I wasn't expecting much free time to care for anything bigger. I made lots of lists.

Barry had a series of tests—pulmonary function, EKG, CXR, echocardiogram, and more. It's ironic how healthy you have to be. If any of his other systems, such as heart or lungs were not in tiptop shape, he wouldn't get the transplant. He passed them all. He also had to get a medical alert bracelet he will have to wear for the rest of his life. It warns that he must receive "irradiated CMV (cytometalovirus) negative blood products only" with his blood type.

We attended two trainings. The first was on how to take care of the central venous catheter that would be implanted before treatment started. All of Barry's blood drawings (out) and infusions (in) would go through the two-pronged catheter. No more needles. The staff explained the dressing for the catheter needed to be changed regularly and flushed with heparin. This would be a caregiver's job. They warned me that the change and flush required fine motor skills. Risks of infection were high and I would need to be exceedingly careful and precise. I was freaked, as fine motor skills are not my strong suit. Since I am not good with my hands—I always break wooden matches whenever I try to strike one—and am squeamish, I avoided this task. I attempted this procedure only once and it took forever. The nurse who trained us became one of our regular nurses. We joked many times in the months that followed about how I always got a nurse to change the dressing. Only one nurse during the entire time we were at Stanford chastised me for not changing the dressing. Everyone else just did it one, two, three.

In late September, we took a six-day trip to Boston where Barry grew up. My company was celebrating its 50th anniversary and they flew everyone in for the festivities. Barry and I went a few days earlier for a mini-vacation and a little fieldwork by Barry for a book he was writing.

After we returned, our first appointment was with the radiation oncologist who explained how the TLI (total lymphoid irradiation) would be performed. He told us that the fields where the radiation would be administered were big and the doses would be low. Most people, he claimed, tolerated it very well. He also assured us that secondary malignancies caused by radiation were more common in younger people.

At our next appointment with Dr. Miklos, I had questions. What could we expect? How sick would Barry be? He said it was hard to know, and that certainly turned out to be true. When I asked Dr. Miklos how restricted our life would be in the next period of time, he said he wanted us to have as few visitors to our apartment as possible to minimize Barry's exposure to infectious agents. He also told us that I would not be able to stay with Barry in the hospital during his pre-transplant treatment.

We learned that the donor was a twenty-year old woman who had never been pregnant. There had apparently been as many as six potential matches in the donor bank and Dr. Miklos had been able to identify the very best match for Barry. We were psyched.

(I belong to two women's groups. One is a group of six extraordinary women with whom I share a political past. We all met during the 1960s while activists in the movement against the Vietnam War and for racial justice. This next email is to them.)

October 12, 2006

Dearest Friends,

... I'm pretty freaked out, and the very last stage of denial has been stripped away.

I don't know about food yet. Probably the best thing, for those of you who want to cook for us, will be to freeze small portions. I'll know more after we meet with the dietician when Barry is in the hospital, from Oct. 22–28. I can't stay with him overnight this time; but plan to stay with our good friends in Palo Alto until I can move into the apartment on the twenty-sixth. The good news is that the apartment is right across from the hospital, totally within walking distance. It has a great fitness center—I hope to have some time to work out while he's at the Cancer Center (two to four hours a day) and I'm not doing errands. Megan will be coming down on Mondays and will be his caregiver while I come up to the city and work.

Right now, I'm very busy making arrangements for the move and we still have lots of appointments down at Stanford. Also, I'm frantically wrapping things up at work in preparation for my leave.

Please keep in touch. I am in dire need of support.

Love,

Bonnie

BARRY:

We'd planned a busy summer of traveling. I was scheduled to return to Colby College in Waterville, ME for my fortieth reunion where I was going to participate in a class author reading. I was looking forward to it, but it was not to be. My Campath schedule prohibited travel during May through July. Then the listeria bug wiped out the Montana yoga retreat.

There was one trip left on our agenda and its importance loomed increasingly large. Thomas Wolfe wrote: "You can't go home again." The point being that however much we try not to, we burn our bridges or that they get burned despite our wishes. The impossibilities inherent in this bittersweet nostalgia don't diminish the longing to return, though—especially with a dangerous transplant peeking over the horizon.

Months earlier, Bonnie had booked us for travel to her company's anniversary celebration, scheduled for late September in Boston where I grew up. It seemed fitting to return to the place I spent my childhood and adolescent years, just before I took the plunge with a transplant. I looked at it as possibly my last trip ever and it came to assume enormous meaning to me. I decided to move heaven and earth to make the trip.

On Tuesday, Sept. 26 we flew to Logan and drove through Malden on our way to Gloucester. My family had lived in Malden since the beginning of the last century. My grandmother bought a pre-Civil War home there around 1910, a large wood frame three-story house that originally had a front porch suitable for rocking chairs, a white picket fence and a lot of land around it. There were farms in the area back then and she had my grandfather build a chicken coop out back, with a cellar and foundation of fieldstone walls. I remember the walls very well, as one winter while sledding I went over the wall and into the cellar, hitting my head on a protruding piece of jagged fieldstone, barely missing an eye. I still have a scar from that fiasco. Behind the house was an expanse of New England deciduous woods—oak, maple, birch and ash—with an all-year brook that sometimes flooded to make a swamp. In winters there was even enough open ice for a small hockey game. Now there are newer homes down there, built over the swamp, with cellars that leak and require sump pumps. I lived the first fourteen years of my life in that creaky old house and needed to see it.

The house has a steeply pitched gabled roof and might have been a classic but for the renovations that my family made to it over the years. There are the utilitarian additions that equate to warts on the face of an otherwise beautiful woman. There's the "upgraded" asbestos siding done in the 1950s when it was all the rage. The front porch, closed in now, has become a dank entryway. It remains in the family and is now five rental units occupied by strangers.

Stopping out front and walking around the yard evokes poignant memories of a childhood long ago. It is 1949 and our family occupies three of the apartments. I am four years old as I watch my grandmother take her last trip down the dimly lit stairs, bundled up in a dark winter coat, gripping the banister for support as she descends, one slow step at a time. I'm standing at the top of the stairs for what seems an eternity, hoping for a glimpse of her face, for a smile of assurance that has always been there for me, but she never looks back. My last sight of her is that coat and wild grey hair peeking out from beneath an old-fashioned dark hat. She is having a coronary; but the doctor misses the diagnosis and allows her to walk all the way to the car—probably into the Malden Hospital and to her death.

Then I walk a half-block down the street to look at the house my parents built in 1957, and I am shocked to discover it's been recently torn down to make way for five homes. There is no "home" on Granville Avenue anymore.

We head for Gloucester where we have reservations at a motel near *Wingaersheek Beach.* My parents once had a home close by on a beach in the town of Magnolia. It was there that I learned to row, sometimes spending entire days out in my dinghy prowling the north shore coast, exploring its small rockbound islands and often venturing miles out into Massachusetts Bay. I'd bring lunch and a drink. I'd weather squalls. Sometimes I'd trespass on a remote private beach that was part of a down-at-the-heel estate some white shoe Bostonians built there in the late 1800s. I had no safety equipment except for a life preserver. I never knew where I'd be heading when I left shore so no one knew where I was. Strangely, I had no fear of death then, though I had so much more to lose.

The second day in Gloucester, I introduce Bonnie to Dogtown Commons. Dogtown is a rough and rocky chunk of land in the very middle of Cape Ann. Long ago, in the 1700s, it was a hideout for pirates and, some say, witches who kept vicious dogs for protection. Certainly it once was a haven for outcasts. When it was abandoned in the 1830s, the last residents left their dogs; they turned into a feral pack—hence the name "Dogtown."

During the Great Depression, a filthy rich know-it-all and wanna-be president named Roger W. Babson hired immigrant stonecutters to graffiti the boulders in the Commons with simplistic blather. Beneath the lichen, his fortune cookie advice survives to this day. "Get a job." "Help mother." "Save." "Be on time." "Keep out of debt." And harkening to Chairman Mao Tse Tung: "Never try, never win." Some of the boulders are well hidden. Others are in plain sight. It is good fun to locate all 23 of them, including one that gives the direction to Rockport, as if it were a kind of Emerald City. It's been the subject of a few novels, including *The Last Days of Dogtown*, by Anita Diamant. I want to include it in some scenes in a novel I am writing, and has since been published, *Burning Questions*.

The next day we are in Boston. Bonnie is off at her event and I'm on my own to explore old haunts. I walk the North End in search of the elusive, genuinely ethnic cannoli. I visit the Old North Church. I find a place that offers clam chowder and beer, but it is commercial stuff, for tourists. Not the genuine article.

The following evening, I watch the Bruins play the Rangers in the new Garden, now called the Fleet Center, not the real Boston Garden. When I was a kid, there were always tickets on sale before the game—no need to get them in advance— even for the playoffs. You could smoke in the Garden back then, and not just cigarettes, cigars too. In fact, the greatest basketball coach of all time, Red Auerbach, had a tradition of lighting up a cigar as soon as it was clear to him that the Celtics had the game in the bag. The hockey buffs who habituated the rafter seats didn't wait that long to light up, so by the third period of every Bruins' game, the top third of the Garden was pretty hazy. I'd come home smelling like I'd been lurking in a political caucus.

This time, I buy a great seat from one of those ticket brokers who used to be called scalpers. There is no smoke in the new Garden—oops, Fleet Center—and there is no organ. Now it's all lights and glitz. They are no longer catering to real hockey fans, but to high-tech executives out to make an impression on a client and to close a deal. The game, like all pro sports, has become merely a backdrop for a networking opportunity.

Afterwards, I walk along Congress Street on my way back to the hotel near Long Wharf. The Saturday night crowds are partying, rowdy, carefree, and immortal. It is September 30. The next evening will be Kol Nidre, the evening before the most holy day in the Jewish calendar—Yom Kippur. In twenty-four hours I'll be in services in San Francisco. In another month, I'll be in the hospital fighting for my life. It's surreal. Physically, I still feel fine, but in my head, time and space seem like they've been poured into a Martini shaker and all mixed up the way 007 liked it—shaken, not stirred. I realize I've been doing better with my memories of Boston than with the town as I've re-discovered it forty years later. Does anyone even call it Beantown anymore?

August 2008 at the Feathered Pipe Ranch

CHAPTER SIX

The Transplant— I Could've Had a V8

BARRY:

Within twenty-four hours my journey back in time has become a sepia memory. Hardly a day now passes when some appointment does not snatch me from denial or evasion and roughly hurl me back into the reality that I am marching steadily forward to a day of reckoning. There are appointments with radiology. Lab work is demanded. I have a pre-pre-transplant appointment with Dr. Miklos, followed by a class on how to care for the catheter that they intend to insert into an artery just above my heart so they can pump in all the juice without opening a vein. There is an orientation meeting to teach us about transplants complete with homework. Then there is a "consenting appointment" where they present me with a stack of disclosures and contracts as thick as if it were a real estate closing, all of which need to be signed. My mind is abuzz with transplant jargon as I cringe and claw toward the impending trauma.

* * *

BONNIE:

Our daughter Nina and her husband, Michael, arrive for a weekend visit. Having them around provides a wonderful respite from transplant prep. (Over the next few months, and continuing to this day, our kids and their spouses will be an incredible source of support.) But we're back at it with a whirlwind of appointments the following week including a very long "consenting appointment" where Barry must sign a gazillion forms plus agreements to be in some of Dr. Miklos's studies. He has a radiation prep appointment, where he gets tattooed in preparation for the treatment. On the Friday before treatment they surgically insert the central venous catheter. Then we met with Dr. Miklos for a final pre-transplant meeting.

He gives us some statistics. Of the seventy people who have received a similar transplant with this particular regimen (TLI/ATG) only two contracted acute GVHD (graft versus host disease) and they were both treated. Forty percent of patients contracted no chronic GVHD. Sixty percent got some chronic GVHD, but it was mild and most commonly dry mouth. He explains that one of the studies Barry has signed up for is a treatment with Rituxan, (which he'd already had during his time with Dr. T.; but it was treating the wrong disease—lymphoma— and thus to no avail). This study is to see if Rituxan, given prophylactically, can prevent GVHD. Dr. Miklos also tells us what anti-rejection drugs Barry will be on—cyclosporine and mycophenolate mofetil—and the possible side effects. Unlike solid organ transplants, Barry will not have to be on these drugs forever and they will be tapered down and he'll be off them after about three months.

It's been found that Agent Orange and benzene are known carcinogenic causes of CLL. Barry wasn't in Viet Nam; but as a teen he worked in the family's machine shop where he was exposed to all sorts of toxic agents. This was before the days of workplace safety and masks. When I brought this up with Dr. Miklos, he shrugged and said it made sense. Not that this made us feel any better, but having a diagnosis and a possible out-of-our-control cause helped.

As the countdown proceeds, I can feel my stress level going off the charts. I need some help and make an appointment with a psychopharmacologist whom Barry had seen. When I explain what is happening, some family history and my own state of mind, he says what I am experiencing is not depression or classic anxiety but "anticipatory grief." Brilliant!! He nails it and puts me on a medication that really helps. After that, I consult with him regularly by phone and continue to be amazed at his acumen as well as his compassion. Now both of us are all set to go.

* * *

BARRY:

I need to find a way to detach from this experience from time to time. Its intensity is driving me nuts. One tactic I come up with is to become an observer. Since I am going to have to endure the process, I figure, maybe I ought to keep a journal. I don't have a clue what I am getting into but if

I turn it into something like an exotic and danger-filled adventure, then maybe it will help me cope. Maybe even, it might be of some help to others. But then, maybe the latter speculation is only a conceit. I decide to launch the effort anyway. There doesn't seem to be any harm in trying.

October 17, 2006—Stem Cell Transplant: 100 Days to My Inner Trophy Wife

I was diagnosed with chronic lymphocytic leukemia in July 2005. The next month, my doctor told me I had something called Waldenström's macroglobulinemia. Then it was B-cell lymphoma. Then it was T-cell lymphoma. Then it was back to CLL and possibly some other things as well. No one knew for sure.

They still aren't completely clear on my diagnosis. The only thing they seem certain of is that if I don't get a stem cell transplant I'm going to die from whatever the hell it is. It is aggressive. A transplant, if all goes well, can result in a totally new blood system and thus a cure. If it works, it will truly be a medical miracle.

Last summer I was treated with a monoclonal antibody called Campath. It worked at $11,000 per shot for 36 shots. Medicine today has become a case of "your money or your life!" My blood counts now are all within normal range, but the doctors promise me that the counts will start to go haywire soon and the time for a transplant is now, while I'm relatively healthy. I have stopped practicing law. I am now "retired."

This Sunday, I will enter Stanford hospital to begin my preliminaries for the transplant. Monday morning, bright and early (which is the way they do it in hospitals) they will begin to hit me with total lymphoid irradiation and another monoclonal antibody called ATG. After a week of ATG and two weeks of radiation, I will have next-to-no immune system. That's when they are going to infuse me with the stem cells from a twenty-something woman who is a donor match and who also has my blood type. They won't tell me who she is yet. I have to wait a whole year after my transplant to find out and then only if she agrees, so I can't thank her personally. I can only imagine who she is, what she is like and why she is doing this for a perfect stranger.

She is doing this as a mitzvah, as far as I can tell—out of the goodness of her heart. Otherwise, there is nothing in it for her. Sometimes I think: Would she be doing this if she knew who I was? What would I think of her now if I knew more about her? I guess it is for the best that we boil it all down to just common humanity. Frankly, with all the sectarian strife, ethnic cleansing, and religious warfare that take so many lives, maybe this is really the way to go. No criteria except a blood match with another human being. If knowing only that saves lives and knowing more takes them away we should opt for anonymity. I don't think I will ever be able to look at strangers the same way again, knowing that any one of them has voluntarily saved the life of another person whom they did not know.

A few years ago, on a beach in Hawaii, I watched an older, combed over, pot-bellied gent promenading down a sparkling white sand beach, a bronzed, bikini-clad sweetie one-third his age on his arm. Then another pair of similar ilk strolled by. At the Four Seasons pool there were a gaggle of gross old farts squiring gorgeous bejeweled women who were adorned with enough gold they'd have to abandon all hope of floating in a body of water as buoyant as the Dead Sea. I told Bonnie that I had a great idea for a slick magazine: Trophy Wife. I said there could be regular human-interest stories by the honeys explaining how they landed their rich old putz. There could be classified want ads, a fitness section and recommendations of places to show off. I was coming up with one crazy idea after another as we sipped our rum-laced cocktails with their ubiquitous pineapple floaters impaled with mini-umbrellas. So it was inevitable that someone would point out that now, with my twenty-something old female donor, I'd gotten mine. My family began to joke about my inner trophy wife.

I hope that she has a long and healthy life, and if she is ever in need, she will reap many returns on her karmic investment. As an installment on my debt to her, I have decided—health permitting—to post a diary of what is happening and how I am feeling, both physically and mentally. It is my hope that this play-by-play description of the transplant process will be of some help to those who follow in my footsteps along the road to a cure for leukemia. My website has an option for readers to contact me with comments and questions. If I'm up to it, I'll reply. Please don't send alternative treatment information. I am committed to seeing the transplant process through. Here goes!

* * *

On Oct. 19, I am at radiation getting tattooed so they can line me up properly when they fire on my lymph nodes with their ray gun. The following day, after yet another appointment with Dr. Miklos, we go over all the latest blood work and I have a catheter installed in the middle of my chest. I leave Stanford hospital with a pair of tubes sticking out of me, a reminder that imminent treatment is a reality.

* * *

BONNIE:

October 20, 2006:
Info re: Barry's Transplant

Dear Family & Friends,
  We are moving to Palo Alto this Sunday, Oct. 22. Barry will be in the hospital for pre-treatment (total lymphoid irradiation and ATG, a monoclonal antibody) until Saturday, Oct. 28. The next week he has more radiation and the actual transplant, which they say is like a transfusion, will be on November 3. All of the rest of his treatment will be outpatient, unless he falls ill due to infection. We will be living in Palo Alto, right across from the hospital, for approximately one hundred days posttransplant. During that time, Barry will be spending his time either at the Cancer Center, in the apartment, or taking walks. His visits with people (who might carry germs) are going to be extremely limited, as infection could lead to graft versus host disease, and we do not want that to happen.
  Please do not send flowers or plants, as they are forbidden. Barry will be on a low-microbial diet (everything cooked, no take-out or restaurant food, no dairy). I am not sure yet if people living close by can cook for us, but I will be in touch after we're settled in.
  We are extremely optimistic about the outcome of this transplant. The donor is a twenty-year old woman, half-Latina, who has not been pregnant—Barry calls her his inner trophy wife.
  Much love to all,
  Bonnie

* * *

BARRY:

"Unless he falls ill due to infection," Bonnie said. At that point they were just words—theoretical and virtually meaningless. I'd nearly died from a listeria infection only four months earlier; but still, I didn't think that lightning would strike twice. I'd paid my full dues with the listeria. It had been a wake-up call for the transplant. Wasn't that enough?

On October 20, 2006, just days before my hospitalization in preparation for the transplant, I posted *My Karmic Accounting.*

I was reminded of a story told to me by my friend, Stan, who volunteers at a hospice, about one poor soul who had a very difficult time passing.

He had an estranged son, whom he had not seen or heard from for many years and was tormented because of it. In the last days of the man's difficult ordeal, Stan contacted the man's sister in an effort to get in touch with the son so that perhaps there could be reconciliation or at least to say a last goodbye. He was told that the son had died several years earlier. It was too late.

I heard my friend's story just around the time I received a tentative diagnosis of T-cell lymphoma—a virulent disease that if untreated can kill within a few months; on top of that, treatment does not prolong life a great deal. So I set about doing a karmic accounting. Were there people I had wronged for whom apologies were in order? Did I have any unfinished business with anyone? Putting aside material issues, did my life add up as a karmic credit or debit? Was I in the black or in the red?

My mother used to advise: "Never do today what you can put off until tomorrow," smirking as she added "'cause you may never have to do it."

I used to laugh, thinking she had a good point; but I never thought it through. You can't get that today back. What if tomorrow you really wish you had done it the day before, because it needed to be done then and now you'll never be able to do it?

I had a beautiful girlfriend in high school who didn't have a mean bone in her body. I tired of our relationship and dumped her without any explanation at all, the way clumsy teenagers treat one another. As I approached D-day for transplant, I had an urge to contact her—just to apologize, however belatedly, for being an asshole nearly forty-five years earlier. It didn't make much sense, as a rational act, but I wanted to do it. I wanted to repent and wipe the slate clean of a lingering regret, not for ending our relationship, but the way I did it. I spent a lot of time trying to track her down but every effort came to a dead end, until I finally located one of her brothers. I called him up. He didn't remember me. "Oh," he said finally, "she died about five years ago. Had heart problems." It was a small matter, but it made the point. Do it now, because if you put it off, it may be too late.

So I trotted out the mental chalkboard and began to make a list. First, I decided to clean the regret slate of all the issues involved in the road not taken. What I could have done or what might have been was just too speculative. For all I knew, I could have been run over by a truck (or as we say in my family, ROBATTED) on my very first step along the road not taken. All that was out. What I needed to include in my accounting was only the things that I had done.

I was pretty pleased to discover that I was not in the red. I didn't have any big-time enemies. I have a lot of terrific friends. I have a loving and caring family—a wife who is 110 percent in my corner. I've had a pretty damn good life. I never wanted for a meal, or a roof over my head. I've had lots of good times with lots of great folks. Compared to the ninety-nine percent, I think I've done pretty well with the time given me. I wasn't going to kvetch about how life was so short, or about the tragedy of dying. I didn't want it to happen; I wanted more of the good life, but I damn well didn't have any grounds to complain, given what I had been given. That made me feel real good. It's not to say I didn't have issues needing attention. But they were nothing like that predeceased, estranged son. It made the T-cell diagnosis bearable.

I go into this process knowing it will be long and difficult but also believing that I have a positive balance in my karmic account. That sure helps.

* * *

Sunday, October 22, 2006, I awake pensive. I have a *Dead Man Walking* feeling. It is not only moving day, but by that evening I will be a patient in a hospital. A predictable, planned hospitalization has never happened to me before and I still don't feel sick in the least. My mind races through the incongruity of what is happening to me. I feel healthy, but I am not. Logic tells me that this feeling is only temporary. If I don't submit to this treatment, I am doomed. And, ironically, I wouldn't even have been eligible for the treatment if I didn't feel strong and healthy. The logic seems muddled—an inscrutable contradiction.

To make matters worse, by then I know that two of my friends, John and Sandy also have cancer. For them it is terminal, yet they are out and about. Sandy is still working. John is functioning pretty well. I am the one with a shot at beating it, and I am also the one who is going into the hospital to face the imminent risk of death. Crazy.

Before I am admitted, we have a lunch date with our friends Perry and Linda, who live in Palo Alto and who graciously promise all manner of support while we become temporary neighbors. Perry and I are colleagues who've worked together on cases for years. We frequently attend Sharks' hockey games together and routinely end our telephone conversations exchanging "Go Sharkies!" cheers. Linda is well connected to the Stanford health community. Together, their warmth and generosity turn out to be above and beyond the call of duty.

Sunday morning is a bittersweet time. Our Sunday tradition, a casual reading of the paper with a cup of coffee or tea is abbreviated as we scramble to make certain everything is in order and that the things we'll need are all packed. I go from room to room, looking around with the kind of care a child does when everything is new and not taken for granted. I want to remember as much as I can about the details of our house, where we've lived since 1972 and where we've raised our three daughters to adulthood.

All too quickly, the time comes to leave. As I walk down our front stairs, I can't help but recall that scene from long ago—when I was four—that's indelibly branded into my memory. I am sixty-one now, the exact age of my grandmother when she slowly descended the stairs of her home of nearly forty years for the very last time. There is no grandchild to look down on me as I descend my steps, none except that same four-year old. Would this be my last time? At the bottom, I look up and take it all in as if it would be. I swallow hard and wonder: Am I being melodramatic? Am I making more of this than I should?

I know that five or six percent of the patients who have preceded me on this path don't make it through the first hundred days. I know another huge percentage suffer from GVHD for the rest of their lives. The journey I am about to embark upon is by no means risk-free. Everything about the preparation, from the classes to that catheter taped to my chest, says: "This is serious." Still there is a part of me that is in denial and pooh-poohs my emotions. And there is another part of me that still clings to my persona of immortality.

* * *

On Sunday, October 22, as we leave the restaurant and head off to Stanford Hospital to begin the admission process, Bonnie, who never gets sick, starts to come down with something. It quickly morphs into a flu-like condition, something that a patient whose immune system is undergoing assassination, must not be around. So within hours, it is clear that Bonnie will be staying in Palo Alto with Perry and Linda until she recovers. I will be going through this first stage of my ordeal alone. (As I am renowned for my inability to process medical information correctly or to make intelligent decisions while undergoing even the simplest procedure, I am freaked, not to mention feeling bereft.) Linda and Perry will be my connection to the outside world during these trying first days.

The next day I awake from a very unsatisfying sleep to begin the process. By sheer coincidence, there is a stationary bicycle in the corner of my room. I take it as an omen. I determine to keep up my fitness and to work out. I'm not going to let myself atrophy.

I know what they're planning, of course. Radiation and some chemo that comes from rabbits, or rabbit crap. I think I am projecting the "crap" part but my mind wouldn't let go of it. I immediately climb aboard the bike and crank out five miles before they begin to contaminate my body.

It doesn't take long for rabbit excretions to sap your will to work out. That morning is the last time I'll pedal a bike or an exercise machine for nearly a year. And from here on, what I am going to describe is the product of an increasingly drug-addled mind, so if you've got a grain of salt handy, I suggest that you swallow it.

October 25, 2006—Burqaland

I am in the bone marrow transplant ward with a cough, so they put me in a private room. There is a yin and a yang to everything. All the nurses and aides in this unit wear masks over their noses and mouths. I was ready for some serious flirting but it feels like Saudi Arabia. All I can see are eyes. I am in burqaland.

I wear hearing aids and realize for the first time how much I rely on reading lips and facial expressions. In normal conversation, I often say "what?" and then I turn toward the speaker and get it the second time around. Here, with everyone wearing a burqa, the second time is no better than the first.

Today, I have an auspicious breakfast. I order two hard-boiled eggs, cornflakes and a bagel with tea; but I get one scrambled, two pieces of bacon, an applesauce muffin, and weak black coffee. I send it back and they deliver the same breakfast a second time. I contemplate lying, telling them I am kosher and can't eat bacon or the eggs if they are on the same plate, becoming indignant, but decide just to tantrum and demand what I ordered in the first place. After a ninety-minute wait I receive it, only to discover it's not worth the wait. They tell me that with this treatment I soon won't have either an appetite or taste buds, so I'm speculating that Lucrezia Borgia in the kitchen realizes she can get away with just about anything. Hospital patients are a quintessentially captive audience. What are we going to do, go out?

This is my third day getting radiation and that monoclonal antibody called ATG which, I am now fairly certain, is made from either rabbit excrement or effluent. After six hours on this Bugs Bunny juice I have flu symptoms, aching sinuses, sniffles, fever, and chills. My blood pressure drops as low as 93/53 and my temperature rises to 102.2. I am told not to worry. Everyone reacts this way to Essence de Lapin. It gets better the second time around, they say. By the third day I'm supposed to be used to it, but I'm not.

They are slow on the uptake here, but after a while they do laugh at my jokes, such as they are. One nurse holding a bag of meds goes through the ritual of asking me my name. I answer correctly. She follows up, asking if I know my birthday. I say "yes." (Old joke—very old material.) She just stands there for about ten seconds before she gets it.

I'm having recurrent thoughts about Bonnie. I wonder how she is doing with her flu. If there is such a thing as sympathetic pain, is there also such a thing as sympathetic flu? I hope she is doing better than me. I really crave her companionship and my feelings are ranging from loneliness to abandonment. I begin to wonder whether the gods have it in for me. Is my paranoia drug induced?

October 28, 2006—Fried Cojones

Days in the hospital involve a series of routine intrusions and you can forget about privacy. There are obligatory knocks at the door, but they are perfunctory. Staff does not bother to wait for a response before entering. It is as if we patients are children, not yet meriting respect. At six forty-five they deliver something akin to breakfast. At eight, transportation takes me to radiation. I'm back by nine-thirty, leaving me a half hour to read the paper before someone arrives to take "vital signs"—the blood pressure, temperature, and heart rate routine. Then there are rounds.

"Rounds" is much like an academic procession. There is the head resident, the soon-to-be head resident, the interns, and in the rear, medical students. They are all garbed in green gowns and yellow masks to increase their anonymity. I can't tell what any of them look like from the bridge of their noses on down, and my hearing is poor so I can hardly understand what they are saying. No matter though, on this rabbit potion it is unlikely that I'd remember anyway. After all that, I might have time to cram in a shower before I get pre-medicated for the rabbit. Then comes the infusion. Then, there is the monitoring.

Monitoring rabbit potion means I get the vital signs routine every fifteen minutes for the first two hours, then every half-hour for another two hours, and after that, once an hour until the bag is drained. While this is happening, an array of gowned and masked health care workers—dieticians, physical therapists, social workers, paper pushers—drop in for little professional-on-patient chats.

Some afternoons I'm able to bust out to perambulate the halls. You have to be pretty thick-skinned to attempt such a public promenade, as it involves pushing an antler rack of rabbit crap and hydration fluids with one hand, while holding up oversized and threadbare pajama bottoms with the other. I have to wear a mask to filter out all the airborne viral and bacterial matter that can kill someone without an immune system. It makes me look like a very decrepit and fashion-challenged Darth Vader.

I have made a remarkable discovery during a few of these excursions. There are some really sick people in here! Now, I know that may not sound earth shattering—it's a hospital. Duh! But still, I have to marvel at the folks they are able to keep alive. I see them wheeled through the halls in chairs and gurneys— slumping, gray, hairless skeletons. Occasionally I catch glimpses of their vacant-eyed stares. Many are possessed of odd numbers of spindly limbs. Faint echoes of their rasping breaths haunt the hallways. After seeing all that, I don't take it as much of a compliment when the docs tell me that I look good.

Last Thursday night, a nurse came in to ask me whether I was a diabetic. I shook my head and wanted to know where that was coming from. He said that he had just gotten my blood-work back and there was high glucose. He added that I had a platelet count of seven! I told him that yesterday my platelet count was 130 and that I had been blowing my nose all day. If my platelet count were seven, everybody on the ward would know it. "And besides," I said, trumping that logic, "no one's drawn my blood today."

He looked at me wide-eyed. "I wonder whose blood it is," he mumbled to no one in particular—certainly not to me. I'm only the patient, how the hell would I know whose goddamn blood they'd stuck my label on? Here I was, loaded up on liquefied rabbit poison along with a cornucopia of pills, sleep-deprived, and forced to eat a high-carb, low nutrient diet that was barely a cut above jail food, and they wanted my advice about the source of some blood! Jesus. It didn't give me a warm, cozy feeling. You've got to keep a clear head, even in a place like Stanford.

And it got worse. That very night, I experienced a burning itch in my crotch, testicles, and the bottoms of my feet—a curious combination, but I wasn't going to let that stop me from complaining about it. The nurse said it was from the radiation. He got me some creams. Another nurse told me to drape my privates with baby wipes. It helped—not exactly the Shroud of Turin—but a minor miracle. Still, the little guys have seen better times. The next morning the radiation people blamed the itching on rabbits.

* * *

BONNIE:

October 29, 2006
To the Birds from the Bs

Dear Ones,

The journey has begun. Barry went in the hospital just a week ago for his pre-transplant treatment regimen. Unfortunately, or perhaps fortunately, I got a cold on Sunday that lasted until Wednesday, so I was not able to be at the hospital with him. But I sorely needed a break, and I got one. I was a puddle by the time we got down here on Sunday with all of our stuff. The packing, planning, shopping, notifying, changing addresses all added to the stress of the unknown medical future and contributed to one mess of a Bonnie. Fortunately, Barry was being well taken care of in the hospital and really didn't want other people around. We missed each other terribly, but quite frankly, I needed some down time. I am doing very well now, emotionally and physically. I'm taking buspirone, which I got from the dearest psychiatrist about two weeks ago and I do believe it's working. He said I was not suffering from depression or anxiety disorder (despite my genetics) but I'm experiencing anticipatory grief. He also gave me some Valium and now I'm feeling almost giddy. The relief of the anticipation being over and the process beginning has changed everything.

I stayed three nights with our dear friends and then moved into the apartment on Wednesday afternoon. I finally got settled in by last night, which was hard, too—involving many trips to stores, arranging things in a different space and getting my computer set up.

I need to get used to apartment life. We've got noisy people upstairs. The laundry is down the hall. Our apartment's got the smallest bathroom I've seen since a Paris hotel we stayed in many years ago, and the kitchen is barely stocked (I had to get Julia and Nick to bring down a lot of stuff); but the place has a lot of light. I found it interesting that I packed up my office with a lot of thought, but not the kitchen. Note to self. But I think it's going to work out just fine.

One problem I am experiencing here is snoring. The air is dry, and we cannot open the windows unless Barry wears his mask, which of course, he is not going to do at night. We can't use a humidifier because germs love the warm water, so I guess I have to learn how to sleep on my side or stomach.

So, dear birds, I do want you to know that I have received all of your wonderful messages, and although I have barely responded, if at all, they *mean so much to me. And Catherine, thanks so much for the cookbook. I started to look through it, and although there are lots of things Barry can't have, it looks like there are a ton of great recipes.*

Barry did have a tough first night in the hospital after his first ATG treatment. He came home on Friday night, a bit early, since he was doing so well. Yesterday was his first day of daily ITA visits and he was supposed to have today off; but he did have a slight fever last night and was feeling very poorly today, so they said to come in. (We are thrilled that we are literally five minutes from the hospital.)

He's doing much better now, and we just did an hour of restorative yoga.

This week he has five TLI treatments (He had five last week, too.) and Friday is the transplant. We met someone in the ITA yesterday who had his transplant the day before, and he looked terrific. Sadly, he was only twenty-seven years old.

For those helping out with food, Barry must be on a low microbial diet. Here are the basics: Everything has to be well cooked (like when we were kids). No al dente vegetables. No salads or uncooked vegetables. Meat must be cooked well done. He's allowed only thick-skinned fruits, unless they are cooked. No dairy, interestingly enough, because one of the possible side effects of treatment can be diarrhea and they don't want to have to figure out whether it might have been caused by lactose, so Lactaid milk is okay. He can't have prepared foods, including fresh bakery products like good breads, unless they come sealed in plastic. I can't buy food stored in bins. Grapefruit products are forbidden. No unpasteurized or flash pasteurized juices. No miso. No Chinese herbs. No raw nuts. Nothing that has expired. It's a whole new way of shopping. No quick in and out of the grocery store anymore, as I have to spend scads of time reading labels.

In terms of food from afar I've gotten different stories. The dietician said the best way to transport is frozen in meal-size containers. The nurse said a cooler would be fine. Food just can't be left out for long. I can't serve (cooked) leftovers that have been in the refrigerator over twenty-four hours—they have to be frozen or tossed.

I will try and write regularly, but don't know how that will work. Also, I will be sending out my regular updates to my whole list, so some of this might be repetitive and, of course, some of this will be deleted.

Lots of love,
Bonnie

BARRY:

October 30, 2006

I had a hell of a weekend. Saturday night was spent enjoying chills, fever, and sweats. The next morning I went into the ITA. The doctor, a skinny forty-two year old woman who looked twenty-five, arrived in tight jeans and with a bare midriff (my kind of doctor). She told me the symptoms I was experiencing were a common side effect of rabbit crap.

I have other symptoms now. My head feels like it's being attacked by thousands of tiny needles. It's probably caused by radiation. All I will say is that I might be getting a little weird in these submissions. If so, blame it on the treatment. Only four more days to go before the actual transplant!

* * *

BONNIE:

Shortly after Barry began receiving his pre-transplant radiation, he started to have pain in his scalp. He accused the radiologists of poisoning him. The radiologists assured him this was not a side effect of radiation. At the ITA they couldn't figure it out for a few days. Then Lenny Navarro, our favorite physician's assistant at the ITA nailed it: shingles (herpes zoster).

And then our least favorite medical person at the ITA, a nurse practitioner, came in the room lamenting that she wasn't the one to catch it. She went on to complain that she didn't know why she couldn't connect with Barry. Maybe animals would help, she speculated, as she was an animal lover. She had no clue that animals were NOT what either Barry or I wanted to talk about. Later I stopped by the head nurse's office at the ITA and told her that I did not want her seeing Barry anymore. They honored my request.

* * *

BARRY:

Well, those other symptoms I pooh-poohed on Oct. 30, that I thought were caused by radiation, turned out to be zoster/shingles. Every doctor missed the diagnosis until my face started to break out in blisters. Only then, when the signs were literally staring them in the face, did it dawn upon the health care professionals what I was facing.

For those of you who are unfamiliar with zoster/shingles, I'll give you a crash course. Herpes zoster is the same virus as chicken pox. If you ever had chicken pox you can get shingles/zoster, which is also called herpes/zoster, because you don't really ever completely get over chicken pox. The virus just goes dormant and hides out somewhere in your nervous system waiting for your immunities to take a hike. People undergoing treatments for cancer, such as chemotherapy or radiation, are frequent victims of zoster so it should not have been a difficult diagnosis, but somehow it was. Right about now, some of you may be wondering, is this the same herpes as the genital variety or the mouth sores? No, it's not.

Before a zoster rash becomes visible, a victim can experience between several days and a week of burning pain and sensitive skin. (This may be a good time to scroll back and read previous naïve postings about when the rabbit crap chemo doctors blamed radiation, and radiation guys blamed the rabbit crap people for my complaints.) Then comes the rash. It will begin with blisters. They'll keep happening for days, all along one or more of your nerve paths. A lot of people get them on one side of their back, or their genitals, or a leg. I think people who get it in one of those places are lucky. I got it on my scalp, face, in my ear and close to my left eye, nearly blinding me. (More about that later.)

After the virus is satisfied that it has screwed up a sufficient amount of surface area to teach you a lesson but good, the blisters pop and everything starts oozing pus. And when that's run its course, the blisters crust over and heal, itching all the while in hopes that you'll pick at the scab and give yourself permanent scarring. Think a month of this torture, minimum.

If you are getting treatment for cancer, have had chicken pox, and are feeling any skin or nerve pain, scream loud and clear these two words: "SHINGLES/ZOSTER!" If you don't, and let it ride, you will soon be feeling pain that you never believed could exist. You will ask to be waterboarded instead. You will rue the day you failed to complain, I promise you. Shingles/zoster gets right to your nerves. It burns them up. They scream for mercy but receive no quarter. And your poor damaged nerves will remember what happened to them every day for the rest of their lives, periodically reminding you of what they suffered due to your inattention to their needs. It is a pain that keeps on giving.

BONNIE:

Barry was on a ton of transplant medications. The staff at the ITA had given us a nearly useless spreadsheet listing the medications, what they were for, and their schedule. There were meds that had to be given once a day, some twice a day, some three times a day, and some four times a day as well as the liquid intake. In my right mind I would have been able to turn this information into a functional spreadsheet, but my right mind had disappeared. Thankfully, our daughter Julia completed this task, creating a chart with each medication, the dosage and time as well as a place to indicate that it had been given. I set up a pharmacy in the living room, and since the meds were constantly changing, printed out a new spreadsheet each week, marking off each dose as it was given. Without this tool to manage Barry's meds and liquid intake (three liters/day), I don't think I could have kept it straight.

I also started going to the Caregiver Support Class—a series of four (only four!) sessions with the social workers in the BMT unit, which sounded better than it was. I sorely needed a support group, but that is not what it was, and I found it to be a glaring hole in the Stanford BMT program. While the patient is required to have a full-time caregiver, the resources for the caregiver were slim.

Friday, November 3:

Transplant day arrived and we were all set to go. It was scheduled for late morning, but the cells had yet to show up. It was late afternoon by the time everything was ready. There was lot of waiting, frustration, and anxiety. Megan, Julia and her husband, Nick, came down for the momentous occasion, and they were texting with Nina, who lives in New York. Then, when it happened, the momentous occasion proved to be a major non-event. It was as if Barry was receiving a transfusion of Bloody Mary. But the cells were in and the deed was done.

* * *

BARRY:

I was blistered and in considerable pain when Nov. 3, 2006 rolled around. This was the day I was scheduled to be "born again"—the day my old tainted and diseased blood would be traded in for a new and improved batch. Beginning this day, I was supposed to become half-Latina. Yet, I wondered, would Dr. Miklos decide to put it off because of the zoster?

For the past week I'd been unable to sleep on my left side because of the nerve pain on that side of my head and face. Just lying on the left side of my head, even on a soft pillow, had become impossible. Every time I turned over, I woke up. It was as if someone was pressing a wire bristle brush—the kind I used to scrape burnt food remains off the grate of my barbeque—hard into my scalp, ear and jaw. (Even as I write these lines, I am experiencing residual pain, as my nerves retain the memory of the insult.)

Dr. Miklos was contrite about having failed to diagnose the zoster. I liked his candor. There was no attempt to cover it up. It should have been caught days before. If it had, they would have pumped me full of antivirals and staved it off. "We'll do the transplant anyway," he said. "It won't affect the outcome if we are treating you for zoster at the same time." (Years later, he would revise that opinion.)

I didn't know what to think. I couldn't think. All I can recall was resignation. I was completely in his hands now. He was driving the car and I was just a passenger. Was it speeding? Was he being reckless? I wouldn't have known. It was truly a point of no return.

I walked into the ITA and was assigned a lounge-chair in one of their big open rooms. Perhaps eight other patients were in their own chairs at the time. Each was tethered to a bottle of liquid hanging from one of those ubiquitous antler-type racks. Each was receiving the drip, drip, drip of a treatment that promised the possibility of prolonged life. A small coterie of oncology RNs buzzed around the room attending to the bells and buzzers that periodically called forth alarms when the bottles emptied or the delivery experienced an unplanned interruption.

For some reason, I'd expected something special, like a birthday cake or a bugle fanfare. I was getting my transplant, for Christ-sakes. I was entering the dawn of a new era. But no, the procedure was nothing special at all. An aide just put me in my chair, stuck a fancy digital thermometer in my mouth and wrapped a blood-pressure cuff around my arm. A while later one of the RNs came by with a bag full of something that looked like V8 juice. "These are your stem cells," she announced.

Bonnie looked at her. "That's it?"

"Yes, that's it. Doesn't look like much, does it?"

We both shook our heads. Here it was, my big day, and all I was getting was an intravenous dose of tomato juice. Talk about anti-climaxes. And for the patients nearby, it was merely another day at the office.

When it was all infused, they packed me off to our apartment. I felt no different. I wasn't quite half-Latina yet, but I thought, well maybe, shouldn't I feel something? My Spanish was no better than it was that morning. I was still walking like a man. My voice hadn't changed. I paid no more attention to footwear than I had the previous days of my life. Is this stuff really going to work? For all I knew, I could've had a V8.

* * *

BONNIE:

Nov. 5, 2006
Update on Barry's Transplant

Dear Family & Friends,

Barry had a successful transplant on Friday—a kind of a non-event, as it looked like a Bloody Mary being infused into his catheter. Unfortunately, he contracted a bad and extremely painful case of shingles earlier in the week and we've been spending ten to twelve hours a day at the Cancer Center. It is an "expected" infection with his suppressed immune system. He's also on a ton of medications, which, when coupled with the shingles and the meds he's taking for that (including narcotics), make for a very miserable Barry. We've been reassured that he will completely recover from the shingles and that many of the side effects he is now experiencing will lessen when the infection is gone. It's just too bad that it all happened at once.

For those of you in the Bay Area, we are not allowed to have visitors, except for family and a few friends who live close by and have been extremely helpful, spelling me so that I can go grocery shopping and do chores. We love the apartment we have rented. It has a lot of light and plenty, but not too much, room and it is only five minutes from Stanford.

We have received all of your messages of support via email, voicemail, and snail mail, and they are much appreciated. Please forgive us if we can't respond individually, but it means the world. Also, please don't worry if you don't hear from me. It's a whole new world.

Much love to all,
Bonnie

BARRY:

It is from this moment, Nov. 3, 2006, that I mark my new beginning. I am no longer completely myself. I have within me stem cells that are burrowing into the very marrow of my bones and setting up shop.

The theory behind a stem cell transplant is that over the following few months, the new stem cells, in my case, the XXs, will kill off the remaining immune-suppressed XYs and completely take over. Of course they'll take over; isn't that what women do? Once the hostile take-over is complete, I won't have any more of the bad leukemia-diseased clonal cells. I'll be a new "man."

But this process is not without risk. I'm immune-compromised. If I catch anything along the way, I'm not going to be able to fight it off. I'm toast. Every day I have to keep to a strict regimen so that I don't catch anything I can't handle. It's going to take lots of time—and no one really knows exactly how long that is—for my body to create a new, functioning immune system.

And that's not the only hazard along the path to recovery. There's also GVHD, which is where body organs get pissed off at the new gang on the block and decide that they are going to war. It usually involves the larger organs, like skin and the digestive systems. When that happens, you get real sick. The treatment is steroids for the rest of your life. I think of what a single dose of steroids did to me just this past May. If the GVHD doesn't kill me, then the steroids will drive me nuts and I'll end up killing someone. Not a great outcome. So with the hope there is that great unknown, and unknowns tend to be synonymous with fear.

Within weeks I'll be told whether the transplant is working or whether my body is rejecting the cells. I'll know whether a big fight is going on inside me that could kill me. If that happens, I'll get sick and probably die real fast. Meanwhile, I have to hunker down because I could get an infection that could kill me in no time flat and that would make the whole transplant process moot.

I look back on Bonnie's email of Nov. 5 and the words that jump off the page are "successful transplant." I'm stunned. What is she saying? She wrote it only two days after they fed me that V8 juice. There is no way anyone can tell whether it will be successful or not, yet Bonnie is doing just that. All we know is that the immediate infusion didn't kill me. She has nothing to base her optimism on except hope. But she's so hopeful, at least superficially. She is putting on a brave face and I need it to counterbalance my skepticism.

I wonder whether it is for my benefit she is making this announcement to the world. I don't think so. She's paid attention to the doctor's orientation. She is more aware than me that the risks and the hurdles are yet to come. I can't get my mind around any of it. I'm just along for the ride, but I do know the score. She's decided to tell the world a great big fib.

I don't feel so upbeat during those first few weeks after the infusion. I wake every day and utter the same exclamation of wonderment that my mother did on her deathbed nearly four years earlier: "Oh, I'm still here!" The big difference, though, is my lack of disappointment. But as the days pass and I approach the critical point where acute GVHD begins to show itself, I have what I imagine to be the anxiety of a condemned man, hoping for a reprieve or at least a stay of execution. "Successful transplant," indeed. What a conceit.

CHAPTER SEVEN:

One Hundred Days

BARRY:

Immediately post-transplant, I'm taking about sixteen different drugs every day. My symptoms read like the disclaimers in a Cialis commercial: "May cause nausea, constipation, fatigue, vision problems, digestive problems, exhaustion, tremors, etc." I have virtually no immune system and am prohibited from mingling with people. Besides Bonnie, my visitors are limited to my three daughters, two spouses, and four friends, Perry and Linda from Palo Alto and Sam and Janie from Menlo Park. I'm not permitted fresh air unless I wear a special mask which means we can't open the windows in our apartment. My diet is limited to foods that have been completely over-cooked so that anything one might call a nutrient (read bacterial matter) is destroyed. This means I can't eat deli meats, fresh breads or pastries, most fruits and uncooked vegetables. Non-pasteurized and even flash-pasteurized drinks are a big "no-no." I can't eat leftovers that have been refrigerated more than twenty-four hours. My daily fare is a bland and over-cooked mush in a palette of drab green and dun brown, except for bananas and some wonderful soups, cooked up and delivered by friends who have to hand them over to Bonnie at the door to our apartment. Although this diet is depressing, the ordeal is compounded by the drugs, which completely destroy my sense of taste. Nothing remotely meets my expectations, and after it makes it down my reluctant gullet, none of it is particularly welcome in my digestive system.

Thanks to my perpetual exhaustion, I sleep as much as sixteen hours a day. My waking time is spent in a daze, as surreal as a Fellini flick. I am unpleasantly stoned—zonked out on pharmaceuticals and weakness—in a space where time is almost meaningless, except for the pill-popping schedule and appointments at the ITA (Infusion Treatment Area). I attempt to maintain some degree of fitness, but am reduced to working out with five-pound free weights and even those often prove to be a struggle. I look forward to my next opportunity to nap and grumble when wakened to cram down some vile-tasting medicines.

Unable to walk the quarter-mile from our apartment to the hospital, I slog through my days, napping mornings and afternoons. I go to bed early and get up late. I can't muster my sense of humor. Bonnie feeds me meds at seven, eight, nine, noon, four, six, eight, nine, and ten. When we drive up to the front door of the Cancer Center, they call for a wheelchair. There are days when the only times I am on my feet are when I have to take a leak. Because of the shingles, I have to lug around a medicine pump plugged into my catheter everywhere I go—which is basically from our apartment to the ITA.

I am hardly able to think, much less reason. Simply reading the headlines in the morning newspaper is a major project. Thanks to a friend, I am able to watch a mountain of noir classics from the forties and fifties. Besides being very camp and interesting on a number of different levels, they have the advantage of running for fewer than ninety minutes, which is about the limit of my attention span for any entertainment.

Except for my daily visit to the ITA, where I get to talk to nurses, and occasionally a nearby patient who is equally as debilitated, my regimen approaches solitary confinement. I never get the opportunity to breathe fresh air, except through my Darth Vader mask. Unless I feel able to take a short walk, which is not every day, I am able to see the sky only when in our car. (The entry to the Cancer Center, where I hook up with my wheelchair, is covered, as is the garage at our apartment.) And it is even harder for Bonnie, who has to endure it with me, day in, day out.

* * *

BONNIE:

My expectations of what our life would be like during our stay in Palo Alto prove to be completely delusional. I had foreseen a leisurely time, cooking healthy foods and hanging out. Instead, because of the shingles, we end up spending so much time at the Cancer Center that there is no leisure time at all. I can barely get to the grocery store. I'm able to cook breakfasts and prepare lunches but dinners are out of the question. Barry is on a very strict low-microbial diet (see prior chapter for details) and it is not easy. In addition, he has to drink three liters of liquid a day because the immune-suppressants (anti-rejection drugs) he takes impair kidney function. That's a lot of liquid, and I really have to monitor this part of Barry's life. Fortunately, I have some great food support. My Wet Birds women's group provides us with many frozen healthy dinners. Another dear friend, Cheri, cooks for us as well.

The Cancer Center is a fairly new building near the hospital. The clinics where we go for appointments are downstairs, and upstairs is the ITA (Infusion Treatment Area). There's a waiting area and five treatment rooms. The first one is just for blood draws and quick treatments. The second two are for solid tumor infusions. The last two are for Hematology/BMT. There's also a back area with about six private rooms where bone marrow biopsies and transplants occur.

The rooms are large with lots of light. Each contains eight "chemo" chairs as well as four private rooms for infection control. Every chair has its own TV and some patients have them blaring. There is absolutely no privacy. If the patient has no infection or communicable symptoms they're in a chair. If someone begins to throw up a curtain will be drawn around them but the audio remains full blast. Talk of diarrhea, nausea, skin problems and other symptoms are broadcast around the room. Many people look extremely healthy, but they wouldn't be there if they were.

Our routine involves daily visits to the Cancer Center for much of our time in Palo Alto. The ITA becomes our home away from home. There are days we spend as little as two hours there, and there are days we are there for eight or more. Barry spends a lot of time sleeping in one of the ITA chairs with a rack of liquids infusing into him. I bring headphones and an iPod, which makes some days bearable. I spend other time chatting with the wonderful nurses who have become friends, or talking to friends on the phone.

One thing I need is time to do something for myself. I want to exercise with a trainer. There is a gym at the apartment complex and I know from experience that unless I work with someone, I won't go voluntarily. Something else will always be "more important."

I call my good friend Linda, who lives in Palo Alto, and ask if she can help me find someone. The catch is that this person will have to be flexible because my schedule depends on Barry's health and we can end up at Stanford on a moment's notice. She says, "That's going to be difficult," as well I know. When she calls back with a name two minutes later we are both flabbergasted. I start working out with Angela, who has now become a good friend and regularly trains both Barry and me. We often cancel last minute and so does she!

Training with Angela is the one "illegal" thing I do during our stay in Palo Alto. Barry is not supposed to be left alone at all. There is a risk of seizure from one of the medications he is taking, but I decide it's best for both of us if I can take a break to retain my sanity and we agree it's worth it. I spend two hours a week at the gym. I keep my phone with me in case Barry calls for help. I am only minutes away, but if he has a seizure, I don't think he can make a phone call.

Oh well; he makes it through.

* * *

BARRY:

November 15, 2006—Occlusion

It is now November 15, 2006. I am not yet two weeks post-transplant and, as if my skittishness needs a supercharge, someone undiplomatically warns me that if anything is going to happen, now is just about the time it will. Of course, while I am expecting one thing, it is the unexpected that crops up.

There are words that one rarely, if ever, uses. Then one day that word seems to dominate every conversation. This past weekend for me the word is "occlusion." (Tell me how often recently you've used the word, or even heard it.) Suddenly, I begin to hear it every few hours.

What's an occlusion you may well ask?

The portable pump I've been packing that dispenses medications for my shingles is the size of a shoebox. It has a long flexible tube running from the bag of anti-viral meds inside the box, through a pump/timer mechanism, and then externally until it gets to my catheter. I carry this contraption around all day hanging from a strap over my shoulder. I'm always connected to the thing, but it only goes on four times a day, doling out a measured amount of the meds for a specific period of time.

The tube is akin to a leash. Sometimes, especially when I get tired of carrying it, I put it on the chair or bed beside me. Occasionally I leave it on the floor. Then I tend to forget about it and end up snagging the line on obstructions or, particularly while sleeping, finding myself tangled in it. Most of the time I have enough analytical abilities to work my way free without having to whine, but sometimes I'm not quite up to the task of unraveling myself. In my mental condition, I can get it so wrapped up around things I am indistinguishable from a puppy. (I am beginning to understand the concept of a leash and to empathize with our dumb canine friends.)

This pump has LED lighting that runs a banner headline above its controls letting me know whether it's working. And once it begins its pumping operation, it also has aural warnings that tell whether there are enough meds in the machine and whether the tube is clogged—occluded.

There are warning messages, "occlusion up" and "occlusion down," which basically tell me whether the blockage is before the pump or if the line is crimped somewhere between the pump and me. I've had several of each kind and usually I can fix them myself when there's an easily observable crimp or I've run it through the pump/timer carelessly. But this past Sunday, when of course there is only a skeleton staff on duty, I get an "occlusion down" and I can't fix it. When I try, the pump's LED announces in protest "set 4" as if it were a tennis match and I'd just lost the last one.

We call the ITA. They have no idea what "set 4" means or what I had done to be flagged for the penalty. They call the pump renter-outers who, it turns out, don't know what "set 4" means either. They report that this warning doesn't show up in the user manual. Jesus, what have I done? Has my pump been taken over by malicious tennis pros? Is this a message from outer space? Or is this "occlusion" a cryptic metaphor from the Almighty? I especially don't like the "down" part of the message. Frankly, if you have to get occluded, it sounds a lot better if the dastardly machine says it's an "up."

All we know is that the pump has begun speaking in an unknown language and is obviously broken. Since no one has a clue how to fix it, we go back to the ITA for an exchange. When we arrive the nurses examine the unit as if it were some kind of rare specimen. They turn it over, open it up and begin pushing and pulling, all the while looking at each other and shrugging. Finally, one of them checks the line to the catheter. When one of the nurses changed the bag of meds, she had to clamp down the line but had forgotten to unclamp it. The pump is not at fault. We had all jumped to the wrong occlusion.

✳ ✳ ✳

I HATE my diet. I crave corned beef on rye. I want *moules frites* with ketchup and a Chimay, a Polish with sauerkraut and Dijon mustard, sashimi, lobster, and another big frothy Chimay.

The ability to eat whatever I want is something I always just assumed would be with me until the end. This war on my diet has gotten me wondering how close to the end I am. But as I lament the loss of the diet I crave, I am hoping that I will experience those tastes again. This hope brings with it a modest epiphany; I am motivated to live because I am motivated to eat some of my favorite foods a few more times. I'm unleashing my inner hedonist, so look out recovery!

There are snippets of optimism that help my morale. My counts are beginning to rise and my face no longer looks like I'm a survivor of the Black Plague. I can send out some emails without need of a ghostwriter, and I receive a nice note from my inner trophy wife. I've begun to plan for the near future—to stay up past eight-thirty. My glass of Chimay is half full.

* * *

BONNIE:

November 17, 2006
To: Wet Birds
Giddy No More

Hello Dear Ones,
This is Day 14 in Transplantland and Barry is finally off the pump that was dispensing his IV acyclovir for the shingles. He is feeling MUCH better and we even have a day off tomorrow! They are all very happy at the ITA about his progress on the transplant. We have been spending long days there, and it will be wonderful not to leave our apartment, which I adore. I am so happy not to be in my big house, and it makes me seriously consider downsizing after this is over.
More good news—Nina called on Monday. They had just spent the weekend with Michael's family for his dad's 60th birthday. I asked whether she's glad they'd be home for a while (they had spent the last 6 weekends away) and she said "Actually, Mom, I want to come out there and help you over Thanksgiving." Made my day.
Being a full-time caregiver is kind of like having your first baby. Barry sleeps a lot. He is in no position to make decisions and has abdicated that responsibility to me. I am constantly busy, exhausted, somewhat worried, and accomplishing nothing. I am, however, truly grateful that I can do this for him.
Being constantly in proximity to a lot of other cancer patients, we have begun feeling like Barry is the lucky one. He got an early diagnosis, the

*Campath worked to prepare him for transplant, and there was no prob-
lem finding a donor. We've been hearing of people waiting for years for
a donor and then dying, or not being in remission, so they're not eligible
for a transplant. When we go to support groups, he's usually close to the
oldest in the room!*

*We keep in mind so many of the unlucky ones. Our friend John (Judy's
husband) is not doing well. We are very worried that he will die while Barry is essentially in isolation, and we will be unable to attend the funeral.
Ed Bradley just died of CLL (Barry's disease). We are devastated by that
news, especially since we feel a special connection to him; he did a piece
years ago about our friend's daughter who had one of the first cochlear
implants for a child. (She's now a senior at U. of Chicago). And we see Bill
Walsh (the former coach of the Forty-Niners and Stanford football) every
day at the ITA looking very frail and sick.*

*For me, the worst of all is dear Sandy, who became like a sister to me
after we hired her as my mother's geriatric care manager. It's difficult for
me even to write about this. She has been sick for some time and is scheduled for extensive surgery, but it may be too late.*

*So, birdies, that is the news from here. Keep on calling and emailing.
And don't be insulted if I don't respond. I love hearing from you. If you
can, call on the home phone as I am using lots of minutes on my cell
phone. If I can't pick up, I won't, but I get all of the messages and they
mean so much.*

Lots of feathery love,
Bonnie

* * *

One of my plans for life in Palo Alto was to spend Mondays at my work
in San Francisco. Our daughter, Megan, who is an acupuncturist, would
come down to be Barry's caregiver for the day, or at least part of it. But
since he's been so sick, I am unable to make good on this plan. I have a
computer provided by my work to keep up remotely.

I finally make it into the office on November 20, over two weeks after
the transplant. On my return to the apartment, I am greeted by a freaked-
out daughter who tells me Barry experienced an "attack," falling onto the
floor writhing. At first they thought he was having a heart attack as it was
really intense, unfathomably horrible pain, but it was on the left side of his
head, nowhere near his heart. They are both terribly distressed and now
so am I. Barry begins to have more of these episodes and is put on more

painkillers and a Fentanyl patch but nothing seems to work.

Our middle daughter, Nina, arrives the day after Thanksgiving. It is really hard for her to see her Dad in such pain. Sunday he has more attacks and we go back and forth between the apartment and the Cancer Center. Dr. Miklos is on duty, which is fortunate because he knows Barry well. We become desperate after Barry collapses in pain while eating dinner. We call to tell Dr. Miklos the pain is not abating one iota. If Barry were simply referred to a pain specialist it would take weeks to get an appointment, but if he is hospitalized he will be seen immediately. Dr. Miklos gets Barry admitted so a pain specialist can see him right away.

Nina and I drive him to the hospital. I'm not allowed to stay with him during this hospitalization but I'm relieved that he is in an environment where he can be treated instead of writhing in pain at home. Nina has to leave the next morning and I am sad to lose her huge help and support.

On Monday morning, we meet Ian Carroll, a most impressive pain management doc, whom we will come to trust and immensely respect for his skill and compassion. He immediately puts Barry on IV lidocaine as well as other meds.

* * *

BARRY:

November 22, 2006—A Holiday Carol

It's getting close to Thanksgiving. Traditionally that's been the start of the Christmas season, but not any longer. It seems as though no commercial enterprise, be it TV, sponsors, or merchants can wait. A month just isn't enough time to hype up the sales anymore. So the "hollow-days" come earlier and earlier. Right now I can see the fake snow and plastic wreaths being dusted off. The first faint but repetitious murmurs of the old standard holiday tunes are beginning to take control of my brain waves. It's beginning to look a lot like Christians everywhere I go.

Well, I haven't been creative in so long I'm getting noodgy. I've decided that this year we need a new version of an old carol to honor America's pharmaceutical giants. (Who knew I'd become such a consumer?) After you read the lyrics, the doctors among you will no doubt be interested in the pharmacopoeia. The therapists will shake their heads and excuse my dementia, hoping (I hope) that it is but temporary. The lawyers will start thinking about commitment papers. Others will wonder whether I have any of the ones that got me so high left over. In answer to this last query,

I offer a resounding "no." Get your own drugs! These are mine. All mine. Heh, heh!

Anyway, you all know the tune, a staple of the war against inclusive holidays. Follow the bouncing ball. Here we go!

> *On the first day of transplant my doctors gave to me*
> *Acyclovir via IV.*

> *On the second day of transplant my doctors gave to me*
> *Cyclosporine and Acyclovir via IV.*

> *On the third day of transplant my doctors gave to me*
> *Fluconazole, Cyclosporine, and Acyclovir via IV.*

> *On the fourth day of transplant my doctors gave to me*
> *A morphine patch,*
> *Fluconazole, Cyclosporine, and Acyclovir via IV.*

> *On the fifth day of transplant my doctors gave to me*
> *Mycophenolate Mofetil,*
> *A morphine patch,*
> *Fluconazole, Cyclosporine, and Acyclovir via IV.*

> *On the sixth day of transplant my doctors gave to me*
> *Citalopram, Mycophenolate Mofetil,*
> *A morphine patch,*
> *Fluconazole, Cyclosporine, and Acyclovir via IV.*

> *On the seventh day of transplant my doctors gave to me*
> *Ciprofloxacin, Citalopram, Mycophenolate Mofetil,*
> *A morphine patch*
> *Fluconazole, Cyclosporine, and Acyclovir via IV.*

> *On the eighth day of transplant my doctors gave to me*
> *Meloclopramide,*
> *Ciprofloxacin, Citalopram, Mycophenolate Mofetil,*
> *A morphine patch,*
> *Fluconazole, Cyclosporine, and Acyclovir via IV.*

> *On the ninth day of transplant my doctors gave to me*
> *Metropolol, Meloclopramide,*
> *Ciprofloxacin, Citalopram, Mycophenolate Mofetil,*
> *A morphine patch,*
> *Fluconazole, Cyclosporine, and Acyclovir via IV.*

On the tenth day of transplant my doctors gave to me
Valtrex, Metropolol, Meloclopramide,
Ciprofloxacin, Citalopram, Mycophenolate Mofetil,
A morphine patch
Fluconazole, Cyclosporine, and Acyclovir via IV.

On the eleventh day of transplant my doctors gave to me
Nizatidine, Valtrex, Metropolol, Meloclopramide,
Ciprofloxacin, Citalopram, Mycophenolate Mofetil,
A morphine patch
Fluconazole, Cyclosporine, and Acyclovir via IV.

On the twelfth day of transplant my doctors gave to me
Senokot, Valtrex, Metropolol, Meloclopramide,
Ciprofloxacin, Citalopram, Mycophenolate Mofetil,
A morphine patch,
Fluconazole, Cyclosporine, and Acyclovir via IV.

Ho! Ho! Ho! Merry Christmas. Happy New Year and, oh yeah,
have a nice Thanksgiving while you're at it.

November 22, 2006—Got a Match?

It is nineteen days post-transplant and once again the unexpected has struck. I've just experienced the most violent attack of pain that I could imagine. Actually I take that back; it was beyond my imagination before it happened. Here's what it felt like: take a pair of pliers or vise grips, clamp them down as hard as you can on your jaw between your ear and the midpoint of your chin, now twist and hold for thirty seconds. That's what shingles did to me last Sunday night. And if you think that is bad, the very next night Mr. Shingles jammed a pencil into my right ear canal. I fell on the floor and my reward was a morphine patch. I've been plenty high, Kemosabe. But high does not equate with fun while I wait for the hammer to drop another time—and it does.

My daughter Nina is visiting from New York. It is Sunday afternoon and we are sitting in our living room talking when shingles serves up something even more painful. Imagine lighting a wooden kitchen match, waiting for it to flare and then jamming into your ear canal. The match in the ear thing interrupts our discussion and, as if once isn't enough, it happens again and again. When it happens in the middle of dinner I scream that we have to go to the hospital. We go right to Unit E-1, haven *for transplant patients in deep shit, and it looks like there are too many of them in there already.*

They diagnose my condition as another attack of shingles. They say I might be hospitalized for a week and they need to refer me to the pain specialist team. Oh yeah, I also need a referral to the infectious disease team. I am infectious.

I am placed in a special room where the air I exhale gets sucked out of the hospital directly into the outside environment. The room has two doors, like an airlock. Everyone who enters has to be fully gowned and masked and these items have to be discarded before they leave my room. The idea is that nothing that's been in, on, or around my body is allowed to get anywhere near the general population of E-1. Now I really am in solitary confinement.

To be assigned a special room in E-1 is not exactly good news. Just being in that unit is an ominous turn of events, but to be given special treatment within a special treatment unit is to make you wonder whether someone might not be already typing essential information into a death certificate. Perhaps they are. But for the moment we have no idea just how deep the poop is that I have stepped into.

* * *

BONNIE:

December 1, 2006
To: Closest Friends and Family
Shit Keeps Hitting the Fan

Dear Ones,

I walked into Barry's room this morning to find that he'd been over-dosed last night on Dilaudid (a narcotic). When the infectious disease BMT doc came in, she said that his zoster (shingles) had disseminated into his blood and could be life threatening. It could also attack the brain. I spent the entire day catatonic by his bedside as he recovered from his narcotic stupor, rising only to pee. I couldn't even talk to my kids, but since Nina got me into text messaging I communicated with them that way, which worked for all of us.

By about 4 p.m., he was awake a bit and I was able to find out more information. I spoke with the pain doctor who assured me that no harm had been done by the overdose. The infectious disease doc said she was encouraged by Barry's response and by his "evolving lesions." (She also gave me her home phone number and said to call any time night or day.)

Then I had a long talk with the charge nurse about what had happened last night, why procedures weren't followed and how they planned to prevent it from happening again.

I was told he'd be in the hospital for at least another week and that means ten to twelve-hour days for me by his bedside.

I left the hospital room for our apartment at 6 p.m. (earlier than usual) because I could not sit there in the dark in a panic any longer. Calls to me were promised and made. Doctors adjusted Barry's meds during their final rounds and promised to call if there is any change in his condition. He may need a brain scan if there is no improvement.

Now I'm home, glad there's no alcohol around or I might overdose. I'm going to crawl into bed and watch some mindless TV. I am afraid that he will die in the hospital.

Barry did end up getting a brain MRI and I was terrified. He was gone a very long time, much longer than anticipated. I was convinced that he died in the MRI machine. My fears proved to be unfounded and the scan was clear. Major relief.

* * *

BARRY:

December 10, 2006—A Stroll with Bob

I am in E-1, delirious and starting to get little bumpy things on my arms, legs, and in much more private places. Dr. Wes Brown comes to examine me. You wouldn't know it from the name but Dr. Wes Brown is a slim, glamorous Asian woman who could be cast as a "TV" doctor. She heads up the Stanford BMT infectious disease team.

I am lying on my back, my head propped up by pillows. My arms and legs feel as if they are tied down. Bonnie is sitting beside my bed, her expression telling me she's a bundle of nerves. Wes says she has to examine me so that she can learn whether I might have disseminated zoster, meaning the shingles might have gotten into my blood, an extremely life-threatening turn of events for someone like me, without an immune system.

So I'm trussed to the bed as if in some kind of perverted S&M game. She pulls back the covers to check out my penis, which I'm disappointed to report is, at this moment, about the size of a cocktail sausage and as limp as a month-old stalk of celery. I've got this dynamite looking woman conducting a detailed examination of this extraneous piece of meat that in other circumstances I've held near and dear. She's looking it over for ugly little red bumps. My wife is at my right hand playing the voyeur. I'm dying, literally and figuratively. I ought to be too sick to be embarrassed, but somehow, even though they may be taking measurements for my coffin, I'm totally humiliated that the shriveled thing is totally inoperable, dysfunctional, and superfluous. All it is now is a specimen—Exhibit A in a zoster diagnosis. And I am wondering how they are going to describe it in the chart. I'm hoping it doesn't get into a medical journal. I'm determined to never give them a release to publish my case study. What do they put in these drugs anyway, anti-Viagra? Does this embarrassment mean a part of me thinks I'm going to make it? After all, what's the point of embarrassment anyway if you don't have to live with it?

After what seems like a millennium, Wes completes her examination. I'd like to whistle a happy tune and pretend that no one saw anything. "What's the verdict?" I ask.

"You'll have to wait until Friday for all the tests to come back so that I can get a proper diagnosis," she says.

On Friday I find out it's disseminated and I'm not going anywhere for a while.

I continue having shingles attacks for several days after my admission. The pain team, headed by Dr. Ian Carroll, prescribes narcotics—Dilaudid on demand. They give me a button to push whenever I am under attack. One night a nurse installs the pain meds without a second nurse being present as required by protocol. She mistakenly programs the Dilaudid for a continuous drip. When I awake the next morning, I am addicted to narcotics and she would not be my nurse again.

I have several days of painful withdrawal ahead of me now to accompany the shingles pain, even as I am undergoing treatment for the disseminated zoster.

I am alone in my hospital room loaded on narcotics. Every time I go to sleep someone comes in to obtain "vitals"—the combo of blood pressure, temperature, and heart rate. Then someone else comes in to take blood. I am drained and brained. If the shingles isn't going to get me, it looks like the treatment will.

Being addicted to drugs is a new experience, but actually weirder is the detoxification, which presents with a lot of nausea. My body seems to reject commercial pharmaceuticals as if they are peanuts and I am highly allergic. Its rejection of the dope is without equivocation, arriving in projectile form, containing the last six hours of nutrition and able to sail five or six feet.

I figure there are two ways to go with this experience. One, I can live in fear of my next regurgitation. Two, I can make some sort of game out of it. I choose "two." I can wait for the bucket to arrive and can call my shot. I am entitled to many style points, not to mention points for distance and quality of content. Indeed, I am quite proud of yesterday's effort; nothing missed the bucket. I have many opportunities to perfect my technique; practice, as they say, makes perfect. No doubt you will soon be seeing me on reality TV and I look forward to your continued support.

But of all the detox horrors, the one thing that sticks in my mind is the hallucinations. They're not the multicolored psychedelic Haight Ashbury trips one gets a glimpse of in period piece films of the sixties, juiced up with a side of Jimi Hendrix. Rather they are colorless and Alfred Hitchcock scary. One night I awake to see a wallpaper-like pattern of black spiders crawling around the walls and ceiling of my hospital room—thousands of arachnids, all throbbing and oozing. They make children's books with little holographic animals that appear to be moving if you move your head. The spiders that visit me move like in these books. As I think back on the experience I wonder if I was really awake. By the next weekend it seems like the anti-virals are kicking in. Incredibly to me, we are getting the upper hand. The hurling has ceased and the spiders are but a freaky memory. I'm well enough to dump the Dilaudid and want to.

The following Wednesday, they declare me to be no longer infectious and I'm hastily evicted from my single. I'm placed into a double with a very sick gent whose breathing sounds like Darth Vader with fifty years of smoking under his belt. Periodically this poor fellow gags and hocks into some sort of machine. The nurses confide that he belongs at home or in a hospice. They apologize for my being assigned to the same room. I get zero sleep that night. My roommate's bed is empty the next morning.

Now that I'm no longer infectious it's time to meet Bob, who will be my physical therapist. After nearly two weeks in bed his task is to get me up and walking. I agree that's a good idea. Bob's a nice guy who talks to me about his vacations in Hawaii. Before you know it I am on a stroll around the unit pushing my rack of metered medications. The following afternoon, after a walk with Bob and his recommendations for an exercise routine, I get my discharge papers along with another portable pump that infuses me with Acyclovir (since I still harbor the damn zoster virus). Upon discharge I still have frequent pain but it's a shadow of the roasted ear canal experience that caused my admission. Saturday they report that my graft is taking. Eighty percent of my blood cells are no longer mine but are from my donor. Finally, some good news.

* * *

BONNIE:

December 9, 2006
Barry's Out of the Hospital and Engrafting

Dear All,

Great news today. Barry's blood is eighty percent donor and twenty percent his—excellent (chimerism) results. He came home from the hospital yesterday after a harrowing twelve days. He is much better now. He's on a pain medication regimen; he is lucid, out of pain, and functioning well.

Love,
Bonnie

* * *

BARRY:

December 21, 2006—Just When You Thought It Was Safe, I'm Back!

Those of you who turn to my website to find out what's the latest must be wondering what happened to my more or less regular reports. Don't assume it's because these past days contained nothing of interest. I can't say one way or the other; I was out of it. The days since my last posting blend together into one indistinguishable primal soup. All I can tell you is I slept a lot, my stomach cried out in pain, I hurled up narcotics and my head spun. Everything I tried to eat tasted funny. It made no difference whether it was day or night.

Worst of all I have lost my dignity. My most intimate human functions are discussed as if they were headline news. I have become a "he" that everyone talks over and through as if I were some ghoulish semi-being that people prefer to dehumanize so they won't catch whatever it is I have, and I don't give a damn. If I blow lunch on the sidewalk like a down-and-out junkie, I don't care. That's what narcotics do to you. Even when they are prescribed, they drag you right into that puddle of regurgitation and you go without a protest, although not without a whimper. I'm glad they won't let me have visitors. I wouldn't want them to see this me.

As you can tell, it's nearly Christmas now, almost two months since the transplant. I've been on narcotics for quite a while now. Without them I would still feel the pain of zoster—nerves, like elephants, have long memories. But I have the feeling these drugs are affecting my perceptions and I'm not a reliable reporter. Today the narcotics are working and I feel *sufficiently pain-free to write something. Still, my stomach is woozy. My hands tremble from another set of drugs. Tomorrow—day forty-nine—is what I consider half way, and I am getting another bone marrow biopsy so that the docs can find out how well the graft is taking. They say things are looking good and I have to trust them, as they are not loaded.*

Next week, if things go as planned (always a big IF) they take me off the pump that dispenses Acyclovir, the drug that prevents a recurrence of shingles. I am scared that the virus will return. When I attempted to go off the pain meds the pain returned. Why not the virus?

This morning in the shower I noticed that my shampoo smelled like raspberries. It brought back memories of hikes with many old friends. I spent a long time in the shower hiking with them, dreaming that we could pluck fresh raspberries again.

* * *

BONNIE:

On December 22, Barry has his third bone marrow biopsy and although the results are good, the donor cells have begun to drop. Barry is starting on the mixed chimerism path. He, of course, is doomy-gloomy and I have to assume my role as cheerleader.

Nina and Michael came out for a week and that was really lovely, especially since Barry was feeling so much better than when Nina had visited a month earlier. I am starting to get out more. We have begun taking longer walks outside and are enjoying some lovely walking visits with friends. Several friends gave me gift certificates for massages and I am using them.

* * *

BARRY:

December 30, 2006—Countdown

Today is day fifty-seven since my transplant. Counting down, there are "only" forty-three more to go. I am getting "short" and fervently hope that what is to come is less eventful than the first fifty-seven.

I have learned to fear zoster/shingles. Several days ago, one of the nurse practitioners reminded me again that I am very lucky because once the zoster disseminates, as it did in my case, it can destroy vital organs. Now I check every zit, blemish, pimple, rash, bump, and bruise like a fanatic. I inventory the suspicious item and check back on it every few hours to see how it is going. Is it zoster, the mysterious incoming threat, or am I into a celebrity appearance fetish? I know we all fuss over some blemish from time to time but this, I assure myself, is a long way from vanity. It is pure fear that drives my obsessive behavior, not something that is hypothetical. If I get it again it can kill me. Every day I take three big blue horse tablets to prevent its return—an incidental reminder that my fear is not unreasonable. Meanwhile my head throbs with the residual nervous attacks of last month's bout with the shingles. They say that it can go on for months, years. Zoster is a virus from hell.

The docs tell me that the next forty days and forty nights are big ones for GVHD. This is when your body says to your new blood supply, "We don't like you. Get the hell out of our body or we'll lay a diarrhea trip on Barry. We'll mess up his skin. You ain't seen bumps and scales 'til you've seen GVHD. And then maybe we'll freeze up his bones so he loses range of motion. So get out!"

I really hope this doesn't happen. I don't think I can handle GVHD on top of zoster. Give me a break! So I am going to be laying low. All prayers, chants, and good vibes will be gratefully accepted. After that I will expect you to be lining up for visits.

Bonnie has been great, my kids have been around a lot and are duly appreciated, but just the same it would be nice to see some other people. Hopefully I will be able to introduce you to my twenty-two year old trophy wife blood. We can say things like "really" and "dude," do twenty-two year old things (whatever they are) and text each other while we are in the same room. Maybe I'll get carded when I try to buy wine. We'll have fun, fun, fun 'til Daddy takes the T-bird away.

Seriously, the thought that soon I will be able to visit dear friends is what's keeping me going during these long, boring days before release, as microbial swords of Damocles constantly lurk overhead.

January 4, 2007—Dos Equis

It turns out that when a person gets a stem cell transplant from a donor of a different sex, he/she ends up with the chromosomes of that gender. It comes down to this; real men have XY chromosomes, for whatever that's worth. The women that real men like to date have XX chromosomes running around in their blood. But then there are guys like me who have had a stem cell transplant. My donor is not only my inner trophy wife, but it seems like she's some kind of Amazon, running around chasing down all my Y chromosomes until every single one of them is history. My docs tell me that it won't be long before I'll be kissing my last Y chromosome *bye-bye and I'll be a dos equis. One points out that if I rob a bank and leave a trail of blood, they'll be looking for a woman.*

This has raised some serious concerns, especially in a mind as drug-addled as mine. Am I a tranny? Is Bonnie now a lesbian? What's my sex? Am I still a real guy or what? I've heard that they've revoked the Olympic medals won by Russian women weightlifters because they've discovered some Y chromosomes running about in their blood. Well, with a little luck they won't find any in mine. Can I now compete in women's events in the Olympics? Wow, I'm looking forward to that! Especially the locker-room banter.

What about marriage, I'm wondering? What's going to happen to my thirty-eight year marriage? Am I going to be "grandfathered" in (not a hint to my daughters) or do I have to go to court to get a "Certificate of Gender?" With scientific advances all this language about "between a man and a woman" is beginning to beg the question. How does one define a "man" or a "woman?" Can a gay couple "beat the system" with a stem cell transplant? Does it just depend on genitalia? Not if rulings by Olympic officials carry any precedent. What would a trial be like? Will the jury get a peek between the legs of the litigants? I've heard that new popes have to go through some sort of visual test like that since there once was a pope who turned out to be a Joan, not John. Seems like what in the nineteenth century may have been an easy call has gotten all muddled as we plow into twenty-first century scientific and medical capabilities. "Lawyers, on your mark!"

Are these just the mental meanderings of a recovering drug-overdosed (but recovering) patient?" Are my gender-identification anxieties getting the better of me? Let me be perfectly clear about this (as Dick Nixon used to say): I'd rather be a live dos equis than a dead real guy bravely clutching a Y chromosome in my cold fist even as they lower me into my grave. (Credit to Charlton Heston for the image.) I'm thankful for the new blood. In fact, I still feel like a real guy except that I am now wondering what fuchsia looks like and am thinking about getting a pair of earrings.

January 9, 2007—My Day

The old folk song, Midnight Special, has a verse that goes: "You get up in the morning when the ding-dong rings. You go to the table, see the same damn things..." I sometimes sing the whole song, but that is the verse that has all the meaning for me right now. It's apropos of my day—day sixty-seven. I'm two-thirds of the way through my hundred-day odyssey. A malaise is setting in and I'm beginning to understand why that ancient mariner bumped off that albatross. It made that day different from all his other days.

My day starts with my eight o'clock meds. After one of three usual breakfast choices (hot or cold cereal or scrambled eggs), I ziploc my catheter lines to keep them dry and take a shower. Then there are my nine o'clock meds. Depending on what day it is, I'm either off to the ITA for an infusion of liquids, vitals, and bloodletting or I'm home.

My day involves the intake of liquids. I am required to consume ninety-six fluid ounces of liquids daily to flush the chemical residue of the drugs out of my kidneys. That's about three quarts. For the sedentary guy I've become, that's a lot. I slosh around and have this urge to put on a pair of galoshes, but it's all inside.

If it's an ITA day, I'll be there anywhere from two to four hours. During that time I try to read. I am improving—a month ago I could barely read the headlines in the Chronicle and comprehension was not even on the horizon. If you were to ask for specifics, I'd just have to shake my head. I remembered nothing. The drugs seemed to have wiped the slate clean—created a tabula rasa. (Actually, I'm impressed by this side-effect. I had no idea they could do that.) These days I can read a book and even remember its contents. I'm bored and counting the days like an inmate scratching groups of five into the concrete walls of his cell.

If it's not an ITA day—and I'm now getting more and more days off—I lift some light weights, play my little travel guitar and read.

Speaking of little travel guitars, I realize now that I actually should have brought my electric guitar and amp. The people upstairs seem to have no rugs. They move furniture around at all hours and then start chanting what sound like prayers. They slam their closets' sliding doors at eleven and get up to take showers at three. (These are nighttime numbers I'm talking.) There's something going on up there and it ain't just plain living. I'd like to crank up my axe and give them a taste of some off-key blues riffs.

I take more meds at one p.m. with lunch, which involves a sandwich and a piece of melon or an orange. Sometimes I'll have soup, courtesy of gratefully appreciated donations. If it's nice in the afternoon and I don't need a nap, Bonnie and I will take a walk.

There are basically two places to walk—left and right. Left takes us around the apartment complex, a thrill, especially after you've already done it four of five times. Right involves a very pretty path along the creek that divides San Mateo and Santa Clara counties. I've learned every rut and I know every tree. I now spend a lot of time looking for things that are different, which usually involves things like new dog poop, droppings and discards of the slovenly, and lost baby toys. It's a game; not much, but it's all I've got at the moment.

After the walk I read or write stuff like this. Soon, the ding-dong rings and I go to the table; but thanks to the donations of many kind friends and Bonnie, I don't have to eat the same damn things. I have more to drink— unfortunately none of it is alcoholic. It would be a lot easier if it were. God, I can use a DRINK! Then we watch TIVO'd programs or DVDs. By nine or so I'm ready for bed. I get about an hour and a half in before the upstairs tenants start banging around.

Phew, I'm glad I wrote this down. It's an experience I hope the drugs will help me forget.

* * *

BONNIE:

My women's group, The Wet Birds, has an annual retreat, usually in late January. It is a long weekend, and for the last number of years we have rented Commonweal, a world-renowned cancer retreat center in Bolinas, north of San Francisco. Ironically, I am not able to attend this year, and my next email is to that group.

January 10, 2007

Dear Feathered Friends,

There is not a lot of news from here, which is a good thing. Barry is continuing to improve and we go to the ITA only two days a week now. He is off narcotics, and other meds are getting adjusted due to some side effects he is experiencing that aren't too awful, but side effects nonetheless. It's still day-to-day how he feels; however, we are having more good days than bad. He's actually been able to read a book, has been posting more regularly to his website, and doing email and other writing. All of his tests are coming back good, and we have been assured that we will be able to move back home as expected after one hundred days, which puts us home on the weekend of Feb 10. I have been getting out a bit more with my trainer, whom I love, now three days a week. She is going to come up to the city and work with Barry and me when we move home.

My emotions have been all over the place, but particularly down this week in anticipation of missing the retreat. One thing I have lost here is my privacy. It's such a small apartment that my phone calls are not private, only my emails. I have received many phone calls, cards, emails, and Sherry's package from the Birdies; I know that I will be there in spirit, but very much here in reality.

In terms of food, we have enough, and will not need another Birdie shipment. For those of you who were unable to cook because of illnesses of your own, or family members, not to worry. I feel like the two shipments of Bird food we received were lovingly prepared by all.

Nina and Michael were here over the holidays, and it was incredibly wonderful. They are coming back for Presidents' weekend and we will have a spa day (at the Nob Hill Spa) with the whole family to celebrate Barry's health, Nina's thirtieth birthday (2/28) and my birthday as well.

So, dear friends, have a wonderful weekend. I am sure there will be laughter and tears and a whole lot of love. I look forward to seeing all of you once our enforced exile is over.

Much love,

Bonnie

My other women's group (some call it the Sixties Gals) came down and we went to dinner. Our good friend Sam came over and made dinner for Barry. I felt like I was in an altered universe eating real food. It was very rich; I overate and felt sick the next day, but it was worth it. This next email is to them.

January 12, 2007

Hi Dear Friends,

I absolutely loved seeing all of you last night and getting out. Barry was glad for me to have the opportunity to be with all of you, and jealous as well.

Today was another long day (nine hours) at the Cancer Center. For the first time ever (I thought it would be happening regularly—delusional me) we walked over there in the morning despite the very cold weather. It was a lovely walk and Barry was feeling great. We knew he would be there for a while for his third Rituxan infusion (a clinical trial working on the donor B cells to prevent chronic graft versus host disease). What we didn't know was that his red blood count was low and he needed two units of red blood—a common side effect of the anti-rejection drugs. It's not a big deal as he's had red blood cell infusions before. Previously, though, he was feeling poorly. So I guess this is good because he's gotten so strong he wasn't feeling bad when he needed the red blood.

That wasn't all though. On Tuesday they noticed some oozing at his catheter site, cultured it, and it came back positive today. He has an infection at the site so the PA pulled the catheter today. The good news is he no longer has a catheter and the infection is being treated. The bad news is that he has a minor infection (they caught it fast) and once again we have to go in every day for seven to ten days for an antibiotic infusion.

As I've said before, this has been a LOT harder than I ever expected and has not gone according to plan. Dr. Miklos warned us that "things happen," but of course we thought that we would be different and Barry would just sail through. Denial is very strong and helpful and it has served me well. It just doesn't always work. And although today was not scary, life threatening, or painful for him, it was exhausting, draining, and things we planned didn't happen. It will take me a lifetime to adjust to plans not happening.

We did, however, give our thirty-day notice for the apartment and will be moving home—unless other untoward events happen—the weekend of Feb 10–11. Strong male bodies will be appreciated.

I love you all,
Bonnie

January 14, 2007
Coming Down the Home Stretch

Dear Family & Friends,
Today is day seventy-two of the one hundred days after Barry's transplant for which we are required to be in Palo Alto. He is getting stronger every day and his brain is working at almost full capacity. After day one hundred, Barry will be able to resume a more normal, but not a totally normal, life. He will be off of the low-microbial diet, will be able to go to restaurants and won't have to wear his Darth Vader mask except when in a hospital. He will not be able to get on a plane until November, so we will take road trips instead.

We certainly expected a different life than we have experienced over the last seventy-two days. I imagined dropping him off at the Cancer Center, doing errands, working out at the gym and then picking him up. But it has turned out that I really need to be there to interact with the docs, nurses, and physician assistants to take notes, modify meds, ask questions, etc. It feels like every time I'm not there, either something bad happens or information doesn't get passed to me that I need. Being Barry's caregiver has been the hardest thing I've ever done but is completely rewarding.

We are both looking forward to being in our house once again (the joy of a one-bedroom apartment has worn thin), getting back to work (me), writing and wrapping up his legal practice (Barry), re-joining our wonderful Saturday morning yoga class, training with a terrific trainer, and seeing more people on a daily basis (that would be all of you) than each other and the Cancer Center staff.

On the medical front, Barry has another biopsy on day ninety. We have been told that total engraftment can take up to six months. All of the doctors are pleased with his results. Of course we're still anxious and want that hundred percent result NOW, but we just have to keep breathing and doing our best to stay positive and healthy.

Thanks to all of you for your support. It has been incredibly important to receive emails, voicemails, cards and notes, gifts, and food from all of you.

Lots of love,
Bonnie

* * *

Our trips to the ITA are getting farther and farther apart. We have many days off now and are starting to feel like life is approaching normal patterns. Crises seem to be abating and we are beginning to plan our life at home.

One of my life's pleasures is planning vacations. Since Barry is going to be unable to fly until November, and our annual yoga retreat is scheduled for August in Montana, I get out the maps, go on the Internet and plan a road trip. It is great fun and a healing project for me to work on.

* * *

BARRY:

January 15, 2007—A Glass Half Full

It is day seventy-three and I am feeling pretty good. I can walk like a normal person and can work out with light free weights. Every day I seem to get stronger and it makes me nervous. Whenever I am feeling good, I look over my shoulder for some Damocles who is lurking about waiting to lop off my head. I can't shake this feeling that something nefarious is afoot in Transplantland. In this case my mind is working out a scenario something like this. You're feeling pretty good, you have no evidence of even mild graft versus host disease and maybe that means that the transplant is not working; maybe your old, leukemia-ridden blood is winning the battle. Of course, the same logic could work equally well if I was feeling lousy. Feeling crappy could be evidence of a transplant failure too. Or, as Bonnie likes to point out, it could be evidence of nothing at all. Bonnie thinks I'm nuts. She says that she's tired of all my pessimism crap. She says that for me the glass is always half empty. Nothing could be further from the truth. Beneath this dour exterior beats the heart of an equivocating optimist. For me the glass is never half empty; it is always half full … of (ugh) prune juice that I'm forced to drink. How can you call that pessimism? But never mind the logic of it; we're talking feelings.

Unlike those of you out there in the world, who've got tons and tons of external checks and stops that help to keep you sane, I can only rely on Bonnie to keep me afloat and right side up. The problem though is that she is going through this with me. How do I know she's still got all her marbles? They say people in solitary confinement lose their minds after a certain period of time. There is some evidence that this is happening to the detainees in Gitmo. I'm not sure I can trust her judgment.

I've been dreaming about the day when I can have sliced tomato in my sandwich. It is verboten in the low microbial diet that I am required to maintain for one hundred days total. The other day, while channel surfing, I ran into a commercial for a device that cuts tomatoes into little cubes. It seemed akin to blasphemy as I watched perfectly good tomatoes that would slice up nicely in a sandwich get guillotined into cubes of tomato pulp.

"Who wants cubes of tomato pulp?" I shouted at the screen. As if he were personally soothing my ire, the announcer replied I could make salsa that way. Well, I'm just not buying. You can get a hell of a lot of salsa for $19.95 plus shipping and handling.

You know where I'm going with this? I've gotten to the point where I have nothing better to do than be obsessed by a TV commercial. I'm engaged in an ethereal argument about the merits of sliced versus cubed tomatoes. Old folks in nursing homes do that. They get medicated so they won't do that. I'm becoming concerned that the next twenty-seven days of confinement could put me over the edge. This is a cry for help. I'm feeling good, therefore I need a reality check. Will somebody please bring me half a glass of prune juice, pronto?

January 18, 2007—Not in Vein

About a week ago the nurses noticed some discharge at the place where my central venous catheter enters my chest. It turned out positive for a virus called pseudomonas so they pulled out the catheter and for the past week, I have had to go to the ITA every day for an infusion of antibiotics to kill it off. My luck again, they got it early. If only I had a functioning immune system. As Joni Mitchell says, "you don't know what you've got 'til it's gone."

Without the central catheter I have to get stuck in the arm to get infusions. That's no big deal for most people. Surprise! I'm not "most people." I don't have any veins on the surface of my arms. They are all down deep under what has been described to me by a nurse as "very tough skin." (I call it a hide.) No surprise to me, I'm a lawyer. We are known to have thick skins. After thirty-seven years of practice what do they expect? That I'm going to be easy to get blood out of? They'd have a better chance trying to get it out of a stone.

As of day six post-catheter I've had three stick insertions. IVs last about three days. So far seven nurses have tried to find a vein. Six have failed to find one in either arm, except in the crux of my elbow, which in my view is cheating. In fact, four of them have had trouble there too. They stick in the needle and move it around. They wiggle it back and forth, hoping against hope that they will miraculously find a way into a vein. They've tried heat packs, alcohol rubbing, and slapping my arm without luck. Sometimes I think they are operating on a lick and a promise, with the scientific accuracy of a water dowser. In the beginning (where have I heard that phrase before?) I looked away—it grossed me out. But now I watch with amusement. Today I offer to bet a nurse she can't find a vein. She declines to take me up on it, luckily for her. I guess you could say her efforts are not in vein, but rather in vain.

If luck is with me, I only have one more round of the game, "find a vein," before I finish this course of antibiotics. Then pseudomonas will be history for me. If that happens I'll only have to go into the ITA once or twice a week. I know I'll miss all the staff there, as it's the only place where I'm permitted to socialize and commiserate. I can even take off my mask there. We'll see what esoteric bug I can acquire to replace it.

BONNIE:

Looking back on this extremely difficult period, the 100 days, and reliving the gut-wrenching fear that pervaded both of us, I can now say that this was the worst of it. There were hard times ahead, but no prolonged months-long horror show that can compare. And we survived. Perhaps having survived helped us in the future when difficulties and challenges occurred and we could look back and say, "Well, it's not as bad as having shingles, or getting overdosed."

June 2008. Turkey

CHAPTER EIGHT

The Eye of the
Hurricane

BARRY:

January 27th, 2007—Short Time Musings

Today, I receive what veterans call an "early out." I've taken a lot of drugs, haven't missed an infusion, and have kept to my diet. I dutifully drink more than ninety fluid ounces of liquid every day. I'm getting a good conduct discharge on Feb. 2, nine days early. I'm really a short timer now!

Short time originated with military lingo. It had to do with being close to the end of one's enlistment. It brings with it a kind of pressure that meshes well with my angst. (Things are going too good.) Getting killed, then, is like being the last person to die in a war. It's top-notch bad luck and you get real superstitious as the days go by. I'm like that now. The hammer has not yet dropped. I am being very careful that I don't become the nail.

I am pleased to report a sign of recovery—at least I guess it's a sign of recovery. I've begun thinking of others. For the first sixty days after my transplant, when I was drugged out, in pain, and wondering whether I was going to make it, I was immersed in self. Every pain, every blotch, every sneeze and every cough was worrisome and reported. I'm no longer there; I've begun to think clearly. Now I have no excuse for bad writing.

I feel the need to remind everyone there is an epidemic of cancer going on within my generation. Virtually every week, I hear about someone being diagnosed with one kind of cancer or another. I have three close friends who are going through chemo hell as I write this. I can think of two women who are vets, big time. Then there is the prostate crew of four. (Ah yes, I remember it well!) I think that's a lot for one circle of friends.

Why is this generation different than all other generations? It can't be because we've lived longer. Most of the cancer victims I know of are in their

50s and 60s. For the most part, we've eaten well, lived far from noxious emissions, and taken care of ourselves. Perhaps modern mankind should return to groveling for crusts of bread, living beneath vile smokestacks, and avoiding any form of exercise except for grueling fourteen-hour work-days. That's a remedy our current one-percenters might prescribe. In fact, now that I think of it, they have. Just recall the Dickensian lifestyle. Who lived long enough to die of cancer? Practically no one, that's who. The bad news about this plan is that we've already blown it by spoiling our kids. But maybe they'll learn from our mistakes, not raise expectations and raise our grandchildren in the Rust Belt—or better still, China.

I'm champing at the bit to see many of you. I thought that the end of the hundred days would mean complete liberation, but I was wrong. It turns out I still have a lot of "I can't" rules. I can't swim or go in a hot tub, fly or be in crowded places like movies and plays. I can't eat sushi or be in the sun. Some say I can't drink alcohol while others say I can have a glass of wine from time-to-time. I have asked our former Attorney General Gon-zales what "time-to-time" means. He said it depends on whether or not I'm legally in the country and over the age of twenty-one. In that case it means every half hour. If I don't meet these qualifications, "time-to-time" means when hell freezes over—as in enemy combatants can seek relief in court from "time-to-time." Well, I'm a citizen and over twenty-one. I've got mine, Jack.

I'm tempted to cheat on these rules, but then I realize that we are talk-ing my life here. It's surreal. The rules imply I can't travel far, hang out on a sunny beach, or paddle a kayak. I have to wait for matinees, when theaters are empty, to see a current movie. (On the other hand, tickets are cheaper and I qualify as a senior, so there's a silver lining.) What I can do is eat rather normally. I can go to restaurants. I can see YOU. I can dis-card my mask, hike, and bike. I can lose badly to David Brown at tennis.

Time to stop. I'm going off the deep end. See you all soon.

* * * *

BONNIE:

All during our time in Palo Alto I was fighting with United Airlines. Since we had to cancel many trips during the summer of 2006, I was working on getting reimbursements. Delta cheerfully refunded our airfare to Mon-tana, but United was another story. They claimed they never received my letters or faxes, and finally, when I phoned to complain and ask for a re-fund, the very compassionate agent asked whether my husband was dead, because if he was still alive, we would get no refund. I finally gave up my battle and was out $700.

* * *

BARRY:

March 12, 2007—Thanks

Over one hundred days ago, I entered Stanford Hospital to begin my treatment for CLL. I underwent radiation and was infused with a powerful monoclonal antibody—all to destroy most of my already battered immune system to the point where I contracted herpes zoster (shingles). The pain was like I imagine it feels when a condemned murderer gets the first jolt of high voltage juice. This virus disseminated into my blood and, had it gotten into a vital organ, I would have died. It was a close call—closer than I realized at the time. Was I minutes, hours, a day away from disaster? We'll never know because, like charging cavalry, Dr. Wes Brown and her team of amazing infectious disease specialists came to my rescue. They knew exactly what to prescribe to kill off the little buggers. The bad guys made a comeback though, bringing me to the floor and tossing me in the hospital a second time. But once again, I had a rescuer—Dr. Ian Carroll, a double Columbia grad (Roar Lions Roar!)—whose pain medicine team made me as comfortable as possible.

That leaves me with a lot of folks to thank for just being able to write this. I would like to thank by name all of the nurses in E-1 but they were all wearing gowns and masks, so what can I do? Thanks to all the anonymous, wonderful people there who pulled me through the worst of times.

When I was released from the hospital, I went right to the ITA and for most of the next sixty or so days, I was a regular—some would say a regular nuisance. Sometimes, I was so drugged up I didn't know who was helping me. Thankfully someone was there with a barf bucket, just in the nick of time. How they could do that with a smile on their faces is nothing if not remarkable. But the fact is I never saw a health care professional in the ITA get grumpy or be cross with a patient. (Or should I say they never lost their patience? Okay, I'm not on those kinds of drugs anymore and have absolutely no excuse for bad puns. But who needs an excuse?)

Last Friday, I met with Dr. David Miklos, my transplant specialist. He read me his rules for surviving over the next year. I have turned them into a transplant patient's version of the Ten Commandments:

> *1. Thou shalt not enter among crowds, be they in the theater, at the movies, or in games of sport,*

2. *Thou shalt eschew public transportation, yea verily even unto BART,*

3. *Thou shalt not touch, even with thine hands, the person of another,*

4. *Thou shalt not swim or douse thy self in the waters of a hot tub,*

5. *Thou shalt not eat fish or meat that has not been overcooked,*

6. *Thou shalt avoid grasping shopping carts and all manner of like implements,*

7. *Thou shalt not imbibe of spirits even unto the fruit of the vine,*

8. *Thou shalt not fly in airplanes,*

9. *Thou shalt absent thy self from houses of worship yea even unto the High Holy Days,*

10. *Thou shalt not whine over the foregoing, but be grateful that there are not twenty such Commandments.*

So, on that note, I guess it's time to give thanks. This is not the Oscars, but for me, it's better than the Oscars because the people mentioned in the next footnote gave me my life and a reason to live.

March 12th, 2007—Better Late Than Later

I have been hearing from some of you who are wondering why I've not posted anything on my website recently. Thank you, I'm flattered that you miss me. But that's the problem when there is really no news, isn't it? The cliché is that no news is good news. If that's the case, then my little commentaries should not be missed. On the other hand, no news could mean bad news. Some of you may be assuming that is the case. Right now, this very minute, you would be wrong; but hold that thought, I have a new set of test results coming in later this week and it is weighing heavily on my mind. It's like waiting for college admissions decisions. I'll post the results as soon as they come in.

That brings me to a possible third alternative: no news is simply no news. Unless you think my hanging around the house, gradually getting snagged into doing little bits of legal work and writing is news then no news is no news.

In lieu of news, my website, A Gauche Press, like the mass media, has decided to fill its site with stories about Anna Nicole Smith, Britney Spears, cuddly orphaned animals, celebrity adoptions, athletes pulling armed robberies and today's long list of drive-by shootings. It works for them! (No, I'm no longer on narcotics. I always think this way.)

I have residual pain from the shingles that may last for a year. It and fatigue are my biggest downers. Oh yeah, one other downer. I put back the fifteen pounds I lost down in Palo Alto, despite my return to an exercise routine and yoga.

I am thrilled to announce that I am now accepting reservations for visits. Please be sure to call between five and seven p.m. so that I can confuse you with vinyl siding telemarketers.

* * *

BONNIE:

April 13, 2007
Barry's Still Engrafting—Not All the Way There Yet

Dear Family & Friends,

This is going to be a long email, probably more information than you want, but many of you have called and emailed asking what's up. So here it goes:

It's been ten weeks since we moved home from Palo Alto. Re-entry was incredibly difficult but we are now settled into a very different life. The "too busy-ness" that we suffered from before is gone, hopefully never to return. We are really taking time to enjoy each other, our family, and friends.

I am back at work and Barry spends most days in his home office, finishing up some cases and writing. He is retiring from his law practice, unfortunately not by choice, but by doctor's orders and for obvious health reasons.

We have been going down to Palo Alto for tests and doctors' visits about once a month. The latest chimerism (engraftment) tests from five months' post-transplant were a bit disappointing. His numbers are holding steady at about seventy-five percent engraftment, so the good news is that Barry is not losing the graft, but the bad news is that it's not one hundred percent and it's not going up very fast, although his T cells, which fight cancer, are at ninety percent.

He will have a bone marrow biopsy, as well as PET-CT scan on April 27, a big day since it is the six-month, post-transplant anniversary, and somehow very significant to the docs. We will have those results about a week later. This test will also start to measure disease progression. According to Dr. Miklos, Barry's BMT doc, they do not treat chimerism and they don't even really know what it means to never reach one hundred percent. They expect Barry will reach one hundred percent at some point and we were told it can take up to nine months for full engraftment. What they do treat is disease progression. If that does occur they would then do a DLI (donor lymphocyte infusion), basically a booster shot of the original donor's stem cells. Dr. Miklos also told us we're nowhere near that yet and he mentioned that, now that we have a Democratic congress, he has been able to get funding for more sophisticated cellular tests that will really help with his knowledge of Barry's condition.

In terms of other health issues, Barry is feeling pretty strong. He looks great and is at about eighty to eighty-five percent of his old energy level. He is taking way fewer medications and his shingles pain is slowly abating. He is now in charge of his medication regime as well as his fluid intake (ninety-six ounces/day). He is still under the care of the pain doctor as well as the BMT doctor. (The two doctors are working together closely and have some studies planned around shingles and transplant.) We are working out with our wonderful trainer two days a week at home and are back at our Saturday yoga class.

Barry cannot go to public places—like theaters, movies, ball games, shul, public transportation, airplanes and the like—where there are strangers, but he can go to restaurants and he can see people. That has been a big change in his life and we are enjoying it immensely. We had a lovely Passover with family and friends. He has managed to stay infection-free so far and we are following the doctor's orders religiously (hence the Passover reference).

Since Barry cannot fly, and we go to the Feathered Pipe Ranch in Helena, Montana every summer for a yoga retreat that is non-negotiable (except for last year when he was in the hospital almost dying from listeriosis), we will be taking a three-week road trip and visiting some of you along the way. We are very much looking forward to this vacation.

We wish that this was over but are getting resigned to the unknowingness and the constancy of waiting for test results. We learned that if Barry did not have the transplant, his life expectancy would have been two years, tops; and if he had this diagnosis ten years ago he would have died because the transplant techniques they use today were not developed then. They tell us that Barry will not be declared cancer-free for ten years, but ten years sounds great to us.

We are devastated by all of our close friends who are being diagnosed (daily, it feels) with cancer and undergoing various hideous treatments. This was not the way it was supposed to be.

We'd love to see all of you, so give us a call, drop us a line, come and visit.

With lots of love and grateful thoughts to all of you.

Bonnie

* * *

BARRY:

April 15th, 2007—Dem Yin/Yang Blues

At long last I've gotten some news. Perhaps I should wait until it's fully digested before I spit it up.

Nothing is happening here. What it is ain't exactly clear, but the chimerism shows only a little progress in the engraftment. It is basically in the same place it was two months ago. I don't know what to make of it. I'm not losing the graft but I'm not getting my strokes with this kind of news. I was hoping for extra bases but instead I got a walk. While I don't feel bad, this isn't going to help me feel good.

This morning, I was on the phone with two friends, one on the East Coast and one on the West Coast. One is 64 and the other is 52. They both have cancer and both have a spouse/partner who has cancer. They both wanted to talk. I wanted to talk. Later that evening I spoke to the partner of one of the morning pair. Then I spoke with my friend up the street, who also has had a hairy bout with cancer. It was all cancer all day. Yikes!

We don't have much advice for each other—just benign stuff like: "If you're tired, take a nap." We like to think that we are somehow compelled to give advice; that as experienced cancer vets if we don't parcel out a piece of wisdom we are somehow failing to do our bit to buck up the newly sick. The truth is that we are all scrambling. All we really know is that a cancer diagnosis is a life-altering event. From now on, for the rest of our lives, we'll be waiting for or going for some test or examination, or we'll be waiting for the results. That's not advice. It's a prognosis. All I can really say is that coming to a place of peace within one's self helps. I'm one to talk though. When I got my most recent test results, I didn't feel very at peace with myself.

I want to believe that all I went through was not in vain. I want to believe that I have paid my dues. I've taken all my meds—never missed a dose. I've stayed away from movies and airplanes. I've gone the whole nine yards and as a privileged, white middle-class American, I feel entitled. But damn it, I feel ripped off. I am not at peace. The glass is half full AND half empty all at the same time. So to calm down, I wrote a song. It goes without saying that it is in the style of "DA BLUES." That means you can sing it the way you feel it at any given time so long as it is not in happy-go-lucky Disneyesque. We just ain't whistling while we work no more. A one, and a two, and a three, and a four . . .

I've got dem yin/yang blues
'cause my graft's in a snooze.
I ain't better or worse.
I got a wheel spinnin' curse.
Will I win, will I lose?

Hey baby, I'm gonna call you on the phone.
Let you know you ain't alone.
Lotsa friends they's a kvetchin'.
Seems the big "C"s a ketchin'
Their flesh, blood, and bone.

Talks 'bout chemo 'n radiation
Fo' da boomer generation.
Smoke dat med'cal marijuana
Like you soon'll be a goner.
Find some peace in meditation.

Cause of dem yin/yang blues, . . . damn dem yin/yang blues, . . . yeah
dem yin/yang blues. (Fade out . . .)

Okay put that in four/four time, key of E major, pounding beat, throw
in some blues riffs and belt it out with feeling. Louder is better. Remember
kids, it always helps to improvise!
It's a nice sunny day. The weather is warm and flowers are in bloom.
Turn off your cell phone and head outside.

* * *

BONNIE:

Our new life is not bad. We take many trips to Stanford but at least none involve crises. I am getting to the point that I can work a whole day without calling Barry to see how he is doing. We are beginning to step out slowly, seeing friends and family—such a treat.

* * *

BARRY:

May 4th, 2007—Well, What Have I Been Waiting For?

Hmmm . . . it's been quite a while since I've last posted. I've been waiting
to trumpet good news, glad tidings, the glory of the coming of the Lord.
Well, don't you all worry now brothers and sisters. None of you have been

"left behind," (which happens to be the place where they did my previous bone marrow biopsy).

I had this naïve hope that with the bone marrow biopsy and a PET-CT scan I had last Friday, I'd be reporting definitive news. To quote some Frenchman named Alphonse Karr, "The more things change, the more they remain the same." To that I should add that the glass is still neither half empty nor half full. And since I'm on the subject of clichés, I feel the need to kvetch once more about the puerile phrase craze: "cancer survivor." It is like those of us with cancer have this need to be talked down to. The minute you get your diagnosis you have qualified as a survivor. Want proof?

I've taken to reading the obits (to see whom I have beaten, or who has beaten me, depending on how you look at it.) The proof is right there. The actual survivors, the ones who get to send in the obits, persist in using the term cancer survivor to describe their dearly departed, even in the damn obituaries. I'm waiting for my friend and neighbor, Ellen Rosenthal, to take a photo of some headstone in some obscure cemetery, possibly a French one, bearing an epitaph that says: "Here lies Mssr. 'X,' cancer survivor."

But wait, I've got more proof. I've been perusing magazines looking for a place to dump my journals from the transplant ordeal. I thought that one of those cancer mags that they virtually force on patients might be a good choice, given the topic. But ever-contrarian me, I ran right into a stone wall. Their criteria for submissions include the admonition that the story must be "upbeat." Can you imagine? No one can ever die in their wonderful, glossy world of cancer. No one can ever have life altering complications. Everyone worth his/her salt gets back on the golf course and shoots below par. If you suffer or die, then, you must be a failure. At least your story isn't fit for publication. What a bunch of namby pambies they think we must all be that we can't just read and learn about the real world of cancer so we can make the best of it. We have to live in la la happy-ending land according to the editors of those rags. The half full glass isn't good enough for them.

Actually, my circumstances currently are not all that bad. The PET-CT scan, and some other stuff they do to all the blood they drain from my arm every time I set foot on the Stanford turf, could not locate any CLL. But just because their fancy shmancy equipment can't find it doesn't mean it isn't there—sort of like Osama bin Laden.

This time around though, my chimerism was not that hot. Seems to be heading south, like a pod of gray whales in autumn. Doc Miklos isn't worried, or so he says. But hell, he isn't the cancer "survivor." I'll leave the details to my resident, glass-half-full expert, Bonnie. Anyway, I'm feeling pretty darn good and enjoying my negativity a whole lot.

Some of you have asked for another song. Okay, already. This is sung in forties' style mellow blues, not a lot of bass; think Ella or Nat. Very mellow. Jazz chords. Try a piano or at least a Les Paul. You're in one of those dinner clubs with Nick and Nora Charles. You know, one of those places with tiny shaded lamps on white, cloth-covered, round tables. Bone china. Silverware. A maitre d' who knows your name and gives you a "good" seating. Evening dress. Everything in black and white. Noir. "You must remember this. A kiss is just a kiss . . . "

I got those bone marrow biopsy blues,
'Cause they never seem to bring me good news,
And then the PET Scanners,
Start to drive me bananas
So come on folks, walk a mile in my shoes.

(Chorus) (Everybody sing!)
'Cause we got us a chimerism.
We got us graphs an' charts.
As much fun as communism
For us old farts.

They stick that big needle in your hip,
Let their syringe take a sip
Of that marrow in your bones,
Checkin' for X an' Y chromosomes,
To give them doctors a tip.

(Chorus)

So pal kindly fill my glass
But not so full it'll kick my ass
An' not so empty I'll want more
'Cause we each get us but one pour
Before it's time to pass.

(Chorus and fade, fade, fade.)

Happy trails to you!

* * *

BONNIE:

May 4, 2007
Mostly Good News

Dear Family & Friends,
We have results from Barry's bone marrow biopsy and PET-CT scan of a week ago. The most excellent news is that there is no evidence of CLL (Barry's cancer) in any of the molecular tests. The not so great news is that Barry's chimerism (the engraftment percentage) has gone down quite a bit, to 57% in the marrow and 64% in the peripheral blood. After a sleepless night, several emails and conversations with David Miklos, we are feeling much better. He said Barry is "in the best possible position" given his formerly "high-risk disease" state. He is way more concerned about the cancer than the graft and is convinced that Barry will engraft eventually. In fact, he likes slower engraftment rather than a quick engraftment because of the higher incidence of GVHD with a speedy engraftment. In addition, if the graft begins to fail, he can give Barry a donor lymphocyte infusion (DLI), which is basically a booster shot of the original donor's stem cells, and that generally works. He does not want to go that route now as it often leads to GVHD and a possible life-long steroid treatment regimen. He also said now that Barry is off of the anti-rejection, immunosuppressant drug cyclosporine, he often sees spontaneous chimerism improvement.

Dr. Miklos was very upbeat. Since Barry has passed the six-month mark, a significant milestone, he will be going off some other drugs, and some of his restrictions will be lifted. We have tremendous trust in David Miklos—he is inquisitive, brilliant, and caring.

On the shingles front, we also met with the pain doc, Ian Carroll, last week and he was also upbeat. Barry doesn't have to see him again for a couple of months—his shingles pain is getting better and we have instructions on how to titrate down on those meds.

So it's time to practice patience once again—a difficult task for us, and particularly for Barry, the glass is half-empty guy. We are living in the moment, practicing what we learn in yoga and enjoying what we have. We will never have our old life again and perhaps that's not a bad thing—just different.

I hope this isn't too much information, but this is part of my therapeutic way of dealing with the rollercoaster of emotions and the stresses and fears of the last couple of years.
My love to you all,
Bonnie

June 22, 2007
Road Trip Is On and Barry Is Stable

Hello All,

The latest results are in from seven and a half months post-transplant blood work. Barry's chimerism is holding steady. David Miklos wants to "await spontaneous donor engraftment" meaning no DLI. T cells (cancer-fighting cells) are also holding steady. He said there is no evidence of CLL progression, meaning there is no evidence of cancer. Big sighs of relief.

This is really good news, especially as David had been preparing us (and himself, as he does not hold back his opinions or feelings) for a serious decline in the chimerism. So we are thrilled. David has been very happy that Barry is looking and feeling so good. There's got to be something to that. He is strong and has been healthy since we returned home in February. Despite the constant waiting and worrying, he has been leading a somewhat-normal life; finishing up some cases, writing, exercising, going to his writers' group, taking care of the house, doing errands, visiting with family and friends, and even going to the theater a few times.

We leave tomorrow for our much-anticipated road trip to the Feathered Pipe Ranch in Montana for our annual yoga retreat. We had to miss it last year as Barry was in the hospital with life-threatening listeriosis-induced sepsis. Since he is not allowed on airplanes for a year post-transplant, we are taking the opportunity to drive, our first big road trip sans les enfants in thirty-five years. We will not be walking in the redwoods, as Barry is at risk for fungal and mold infections, but as Ronald Reagan (who could ever imagine that we'd have a worse president than Reagan?) said when speaking against the creation of the Redwood National Park," . . . a tree is a tree. How many more do you need to look at?" And it's true, we have seen more than one redwood in our day. But in answer to his question, I'd say "As many as we can." We are very much looking forward to seeing some of you along the way and some of you at the retreat. We will be electronically leashed via Barry's laptop and our cell phones, so please keep in touch.

My love to you all,
Bonnie

Many of my emails have technical medical language, which is difficult to understand. It's the way David Miklos talks. Although I take notes, I can only barely understand what he says. Same with Barry. He's on such a higher level than us. The nurses in the ITA hold him in awe and declare him the smartest doc in the BMT program. We've met all of them at one time or another, and while we trust and have respect for each and every one of them, we feel very blessed to have David Miklos as Barry's doc. We are aware that he trolls the test results and is always on the lookout for Barry. Since I can't give an example of his speech, I can demonstrate his style with the following paragraph, one of five on his Stanford profile page describing his "Current Research Interests":

> *Allogeneic hematopoietic stem cell transplantation (HSCT) can cure hematologic malignancies. Beneficial alloimmune responses target mHA expressed on hematopoietic tumor cells resulting in graft versus leukemia (GVL) and contribute to the eradication of malignant cells following transplantation. However, when donor T cells target mHA expressed by normal recipient tissues, patients suffer graft-versus-host disease (GVHD). A more extensive characterization of human mHA will establish which mHA mediate GVHD and/or GVL. Thus far, mHA identification has relied on allo-reactive T cells. However, our research has demonstrated that HSCT patients develop clinically relevant allogeneic B cell responses.*

Whew!

October 5, 2007
To: Wet Birds

Dearies,

We got results on Tuesday from Barry's last blood work. His chimerism (engraftment) has gone down from fifty-eight percent in mid-August to forty-five percent. Some B cells have grown but it is unclear whether they are donor B cells or CLL cells. Dr. Miklos (and both of us) feel that Barry is losing the graft so things are happening.

Tuesday Barry will have a bone marrow biopsy because more can be understood by looking at the marrow than by looking at peripheral blood (like what are those B cells anyway?). Results won't be in until sometime the next week. He will also have a CT scan—insurance denied another PET-CT scan, but the doctor says he'll get what he needs from the CT. Then he will decide how much DLI (donor lymphocyte infusion) to give Barry. He doesn't want to give him too little and have him lose the graft and have disease progression, and he doesn't want to give him too much and bring on GVHD, which can be very ugly. So, once again, we are reeling. Despite the fact that Barry looks and feels healthy and strong the CLL may be coming back, and if it does it will come back very aggressively.

This has been a very difficult week for the two of us. Barry does not want to talk about this with anyone. Please do not call or communicate with him. I can talk, but only when he is not in the room. This is his way of dealing with it—definitely not mine. And if we see any of you, which we will be doing soon, please don't talk to him about cancer. It's just been all cancer all the time and he can't take it. We did go to our wonderful therapist today and he was very helpful.

Barry does know that I am writing to you; the gag rule got lifted a bit. The only other people who know are our kids, of course, my brother and cousin (I was in LA for work when we got the results), and my other women's group, which is still reeling from John's death.

With a heavy heart,
Bonnie

Once again I was the cheerleader to Barry's doom and gloom.

November 3, 2007
One-Year Post Transplant Update

Dear Family & Friends,
As some of you know, we have been on pins and needles (or worse) for the last month or so since we found out that recent results indicate that Barry is losing his graft. He is experiencing "mixed chimerism," which means that both his blood and his marrow are partially donor (his inner trophy wife) and partially recipient (Barry). And the percentage is going down, not a good trend. The good news is that there is no evidence of cancer and Barry is feeling good and looking well.

I will spare you the complex cellular analysis that Dr. Miklos explains to us in emails and in person, and which is extremely difficult to understand, but here is the strategy we decided on together as of yesterday's visit to Stanford.

We have agreed that Barry will not receive DLI (donor lymphocyte infusion—essentially a booster shot of the donor's stem cells) unless there is one of two indicators, which are not yet occurring.

· *Evidence of disease progression*
· *T cell collapse (Barry's T cells, which fight cancer, have been holding steady at well over eighty percent.)*

The major reason not to give DLI precipitously is that it can cause serious GVHD and that is not at all desirable.

Barry will have his chimerism tested once a month, so that if there is precipitous drop in the percentages we will re-assess. He will also have a PET-CT scan in about a month, or whenever David can convince Blue

Shield to cover it, to verify that there is no Richter's transformation (where cancer mutates), a common complication after a transplant.

Dr. Miklos has been extremely open with us and has told us just how much they don't know. In fact, at Mass. General, which has the most similar BMT program to Stanford's, they believe that mixed chimerism is a good thing. Go figure.

The bottom line is that right now there is no cancer and that is excellent.

As of today, Barry is off more drugs and is also allowed to travel, so we will be going to Maui November 11–16, a trip we postponed twice because of treatment regimens.

Many of you have asked how we are doing and hoping to hear that everything is just fine and Barry's health is not at risk. That day may come, but it is years away.

We've had a lot of ups and downs over the last couple of years, but today we are doing very well. We are enjoying our life, making limited plans for the future and celebrating the present. We are also celebrating the fortieth anniversary of our first date tomorrow, November 4. That night we went to see "Battle of Algiers" and H. Rap Brown was there. What a long time ago that was. But we're still here and kicking, and we still believe in peace and justice. And there's another horrific war to stop.

My love to you all,

Bonnie

The next months were fairly uneventful medically, but not personally. We were settling into our post-transplant life and actually making plans.

* * *

BARRY:

It is 2008 and I am feeling pretty good. I am practicing law again, preparing for my biggest, and last trial, a class action lawsuit by Alameda County tenants against a predatory landlord who doesn't believe he has any obligation to refund security deposits. I begin to see glimpses of my previous life and the near-death experiences of my recent medical history are starting to fade into a nearly fictitious biography. I am back to working out and back to yoga.

* * *

BONNIE:

February 10, 2008
News (not all health finally) from the Willdorfs

Dear Family and Friends,
    Happy belated New Year to all of you. We are hoping that this will be a healthy and joy-filled year for all. This momentous (more about that later) year has begun well for us. Barry has just published an article in an online journal about his step-grandmother, a heroine of the French Resistance during World War II. Check it out at http://www.jewishmag.com/121mag/ petite-mama/petite-mama.htm.
    On the health front, the year started out well. We met with Dr. Miklos on January 4, and made the decision not to have any more testing done until May 2, eighteen months post-transplant. The most recent test results show the graft staying steady at around fifty percent Barry and fifty percent donor. The good news is that Dr. Miklos has pronounced that Barry is in complete remission. They cannot find any cancer cells, and we are all celebrating that. He feels strongly that constant testing will drive us all crazy and that as long as Barry is feeling and looking well, which he is, there is no need for this kind of (warrantless) surveillance.
    Barry is now in an active email correspondence with his donor. She is a lovely young woman and we are all looking forward to meeting her in person one day. It turns out she is half Ashkenazi Jewish and half Mexican, which was quite a surprise to us. So Barry is now one-quarter Latina. Go figure.
    The year 2008 marks a lot of milestones in our lives. I turn sixty (yikes!) later this month and we're going to Jamaica to celebrate with our three daughters, two sons-in-law and one fiancée. So, if we are out of touch from Feb. 15 to the 23, you'll understand why. April marks the fortieth anniversary of the Columbia Strike and we will be in New York to commemorate those events, which were so very meaningful to us. Recognize the handsome young fellow second from the right on the ledge of Low Library in April 1968?
    And in June, Barry and I celebrate our fortieth anniversary with a trip to Turkey.
    We are enjoying living our life in a more normal yet quieter mode, working out twice a week with our terrific personal trainer, going to our wonderful Saturday morning yoga class, spending a lot of time at home,

and resuming a much more limited social and cultural life with friends.
   Love to all,
   Bonnie

Doing the research and discovering that this woman that he knew virtually nothing about, even though she was married to his grandfather from when he was four years old until his grandfather died when he was seventeen years old, was very meaningful to him. Here's a quote from the article:

> *From 1941 through the liberation of Paris, this diminutive, middle-aged, Jewish mother had been a fighter in the Maquis, rising to command a communications and supply unit. During that time, she saw death close up. She participated in two of the most daring operations undertaken by the Maquis in Paris. She crossed German lines innumerable times, transporting Jewish children to the relative safety of the Vichy zone. She lost her husband and two children—who were also combatants. And then, after liberation, she made many more painful trips south to recover these children.*

May 22, 2008
Short Note with Good News

Dear Family and Friends,

   On May 2, eighteen months post-transplant, Barry had a bone marrow biopsy and a PET-CT Scan. Dr. Miklos emailed us the results: "no CLL" just a "few old shoddy lymph nodes."
   When we met with David in May, he was very happy about Barry's health and not at all concerned about the graft. He said it is likely Barry will continue with a mixed chimerism and that's fine with him as long as there is no cancer. The results of the chimerism came in yesterday and it is still low. So, bottom line, Barry has no cancer, feels (and looks) great, and he fought off a nasty infection about a month ago. We don't have to go back to Stanford for another six months! If the doctor is happy, we're happy.
   We head off to Turkey next week to celebrate our fortieth anniversary, a trip that did not become completely real until May 2.
   Many of you have told me how much you appreciate my emails as a way of keeping you updated and in touch. This one-way correspondence has helped me as well, to put into words, almost in real time, the process

we are in, the feelings we are experiencing, and the connection with all of you. Your love and support has meant everything. We could not have made it without all of you and we are very grateful.

Much love to all,

Bonnie

* * *

BARRY:

In June 2008, we travelled to Turkey to celebrate our fortieth anniversary. We sailed from Antalya up the coast, stopping in pristine coves, exploring ruins from Hittite to Ottoman, and soared in a colorful balloon over Cappadocia. We dined sumptuously high above the Bosporus, looking out on Hagia Sophia, the Blue Mosque, and the Golden Horn. We experienced magical moments and life was good to us.

In October 2008, I began the BIG trial—a class action suit against a major Oakland landlord who makes it a practice to not refund security deposits to his tenants. I spent nearly a month sitting at a counsel table elbow to elbow with the miscreant. The jury brought in a verdict against him for over five and a half million dollars. Some jurors wanted to penalize him even more. We were thrilled. On the very same night, Obama was elected president. It looked like a new beginning. Immediately after, though, I was exhausted. I needed a nap every day. I could hardly read. It was pretty clear that I couldn't try cases anymore. I was sick for a whole month.

But a cloud passes over the silver lining of the October and November good news. Our dear friend, Gus Reichbach, a judge in New York, has been diagnosed with pancreatic cancer. He is such a strong, vibrant character, it is the last thing I expected to happen to him. If cancer can hit Gus, it can hit anybody.

* * *

BONNIE:

November 7, 2008
Good News Week Personally as well as Globally

Dear Family and Friends,
Barry won his "last trial ever"—a class action against an evil Oakland landlord. The jury hated the guy, with good reason, and awarded the tenants five point six million dollars!!! Barry feels so gratified that his last

case was meaningful and so successful.

Last Friday Barry had his two-year post-transplant biopsy and CT scan. We had a great meeting with David and he said that he didn't think it was significant if Barry loses the graft, which for us has been the scariest question to ask. Yesterday we got the following email from David Miklos, Barry's BMT doc:

> *Hi Barry and Bonnie,*
> *Your T cell donor chimerism are mixed but stable. Your neu-trophils seem to be decreasing. Still the bone marrow biopsy with flow cytometry was negative as were your CT scans. We cannot find a cancer clone. So in summary, you're in remission, you tried your last case, OBAMA won. Pretty good news.*
> *David*

Still sobbing with joy about Obama's massive and historic victory. Not happy about Prop. Eight, but history is on our side.
With love and joy,
Bonnie

In November 2008 our first grandchild is born: a healthy daughter, Mimi, to our middle daughter, Nina, and her husband Michael. We have made it to see a grandchild! Who would have guessed we'd have been so blessed?

I would not write again for another year, when things began to fall apart once again.

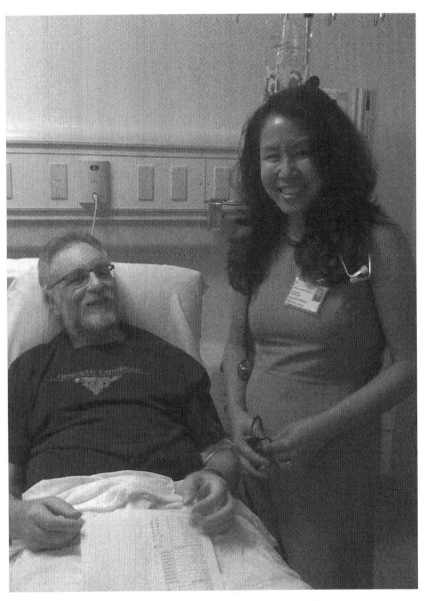

June 2010. At Stanford with Dr. Wes Brown

CHAPTER NINE

Second Bite at the Apple

BARRY:

May 1, 2010—Second Bite at the Apple

I get a little cocky. My transplant is nearly three years in the past, and although I am losing the graft, I say to myself: "Who needs it, I'm feeling fine."

We go back to yoga camp. In August, Bonnie and I hike in the Sierra Nevada, the Desolation Wilderness, where there is still snow on the ground. The air is thin and brisk. I am inhaling the familiar, seductive scents of alpine forest. My ears fill with the murmurs of falling water. I am none the worse for wear after about eight miles of up and down, except for an extremely poor estimate of the amount of water we'd consume. Blood, good wholesome blood, I think, is flowing in my veins. It's not necessarily all my donor's blood, but it seems like pretty damn good blood all the same. We were daring to assume that we'd gotten our old life back—a big mistake.

In October, I travel to D.C. for a conference. Shortly after I return it is time for my semi-annual blood tests. Oops. There is a teeny tiny problem. It seems like my platelets (the little guys that stop bleeding) are way too low. Indeed, they are half of low normal. It has to be either a mistake or some type of infection. It can't be anything serious, certainly. I am still feeling fine. We decide to retest.

Just before Thanksgiving, I get the retest results. The platelet count is now even lower, only one-third of low normal. Something is up. Dr. Miklos opines that maybe it is a result of losing my graft. I have a bone marrow biopsy that confirms the loss of most of the graft.

Dr. Miklos prescribes steroids but they don't work. Then he tries Rituxan, which also strikes out. He says it is now time to think about a DLI "boost." But for DLI, I needed to get more cells from my intrepid donor, Jennifer.

* * *

BONNIE:

Dec. 9, 2009
Not Good News About Barry's Health

Dear Family & Friends,
    As some of you know, Barry's platelets have been dropping. We found this out as a result of his three-year post-transplant regular blood work in November. Since then, he has had a PET-CT scan and a bone marrow biopsy, which ruled out a reoccurrence of his cancer (CLL). That's the good news.
    The platelets have now dropped to 22,000. Normal is 140,000–400,000. Doctor Miklos does not think that this is ITP (idiopathic thrombocytopenic purpura) but rather is a result of Barry losing his graft.
    Barry has started on heavy-duty steroids today and may do two courses, but David is not optimistic about this treatment. (We are also grieving that Barry will no longer be able to compete in the Olympics.)
    He is planning on giving Barry an infusion of his donor's cells in January. This is not the donor lymphocyte infusion (DLI) that he told us about earlier but a different kind of infusion that he has to get from the donor. She will have to go through some light chemo and apheresis again. We hope that she is willing and able to do that. It will take time, hence January. It will just be a normal, if you can call anything about this normal, infusion—no hideous prep like for the transplant. If for some reason the donor's cells are not available, Barry will get the DLI with the cells from the original transplant, which they save. Don't ask me what the difference is.
    This is all terribly confusing and distressing. David just got back from the ASH (American Society of Hematology) conference in New Orleans where he consulted with many of his colleagues about Barry's unusual situation. We all knew Barry was a unique individual, but who needs him to have a unique (and terrifying) condition? And we thought that we were approaching the exit from the damned woods.
    Tonight we go to our wonderful book group where we are reading the cheery, but amazing Slaughterhouse Five.
    I will keep you posted as we know more.
    Love,
    Bonnie

Dec. 20, 2009
Platelets Up/Platelets Down—The Roller Coaster Ride Continues

Dear Family & Friends,

Since I last wrote to you, about ten days ago, many things have happened, some good, some not so good.

On the good side: Barry responded to the steroids. We had been told there was a fifty-fifty chance of response, so this is very good news. Barry's donor is completely on board for donating stem cells again for his "boost." It is scheduled for January 21. This woman is a saint. It is not insignificant for her to do this but she is not hesitating one bit. She and Barry had not been in touch since last summer, but she friended him on Facebook when she was notified about the need for a new donation.

We have full confidence in the team at Stanford. Every time we go in (which has been very frequent lately) nurses and other doctors praise David Miklos unconditionally. This is a huge relief. He's a really smart and caring man.

On the not so good side:

Barry ended up in the hospital last Monday night with RSV (respiratory syncytial virus). He only was in overnight (big relief) and is now finished with his course of heavy-duty anti-viral meds (Ribavirin), which made him high but not the good kind of high. Because the CT scan he got Monday night was clear, he was sent home with oral meds and did not have to have Ribavirin administered as an aerosol while being tented, which does not sound like fun at all. The platelets continue to drop when Barry is not in treatment. He is manufacturing platelets but antibodies are zapping them. His infectious disease doc, Wes Brown (more about her later) describes this as teenagers gone wild.

Tuesday he starts on a four-week course of rituximab, the monoclonal antibody that hasn't worked on Barry for anything so far.

The January 21 "boost" of his donor's cells will have fewer T cells than the original transplant for reasons only David Miklos can explain to other doctors but not to us ordinary folks. If the boost does not work, they can still give Barry DLI from the cells that they saved from the original transplant.

David has told us that they will never know the reason for his ITP (idiopathic thrombocytopenic purpura). It is an autoimmune disease and could have been from a virus, or could be from his mixed chimerism. About five percent of post-transplant patients get this. He does have another patient with a similar mixed chimerism who had this treatment and he is doing great.

In the midst of this, our insurance company denied authorization for outpatient Ribavirin pills so we had to go to Stanford on Wednesday, and I had to take three hours of sick time because they would have rather him stay in the hospital than cover the measly amount (about $200). They finally authorized it on Thursday and we have been reimbursed. Today, when we saw the amazing Wes Brown (infectious disease doc with the BMT program who saved Barry's life when he had disseminated zoster three years ago) she and I commiserated about our fights with Blue Shield. At one point I had someone at Blue Shield tell me that since Barry had not authorized me to talk to them they couldn't tell me anything. I had a major meltdown, not helped by the understanding that we are among the lucky ones who have "good" health insurance while the US Senate dithers away.

So we're back in it. We had begun to live a "normal" life, not without some trepidation, but making nice plans. We will still be able to go to Palm Springs with our family, including our adorable granddaughter Mimi over the holidays, but we have canceled a trip to Africa in March. "Too risky," says David Miklos, and we agree.

I have also re-assumed my role as family cheerleader. When Barry gets down, which, for those of you who know him well, is not infrequent, it is up to me, no matter how I feel, to relate the facts and try and make him feel better. I never lie to him but I do sometimes have to pretend hope that is difficult to muster.

As always, we appreciate your notes, emails and calls. Please forgive the length of this email and the confusing medical details. It's my reaction to my re-activated PTSD.

Wishing everyone a healthy and happy holiday season. Let's hope 2010 is a banner year.

Love,

Bonnie

* * *

BARRY:

My donor, Jennifer, has been a real blessing and we've had a fulfilling email exchange since approximately a year after my transplant when the powers-that-be allowed us to learn each other's true identities. I hated to impose, but Doc Miklos said that the DLI "boost" required another donation from her. So they called her up and asked. She told them that of course she would help, but wasn't there some rule they had that donors couldn't be pregnant? "Yes," they said. And she said something like,

"Wow, you just caught me in the nick of time. My husband and I were planning to start trying next month!" Incredibly, she volunteered to hold off until after another donation of stem cells, which happened the second week of January 2010.

Meanwhile, we got to spend a wonderful family getaway in Palm Springs with complete family including in-laws; but the star of the show was my one-year old granddaughter, Mimi. Unfortunately, I was pretty fatigued and had to nap a lot. My blood was obviously screwed up. I began having nosebleeds that forced me to the local emergency room one night because it wouldn't stop. I also began bleeding from my gums. What was going on?

* * *

BONNIE:

Jan. 26, 2010
Boost Postponed—Moving to Plan B

Dear Family & Friends,
    What a month! Barry was being treated with rituximab and dexamethasone for his ITP (idiopathic thrombocytopenic purpura), low platelets, and he was miserable (fatigue, dizziness, headaches and sleeplessness), plus they were not effective. He had two serious bleeding episodes. One sent him to the ER in Palm Springs in the dead of the night with an uncontrollable nosebleed. Fortunately, it wasn't a big city hospital so he was seen quickly. The other brought us to Stanford with spontaneous bleeding from the gums.
    The labs showed that Barry has a multitude of large granular lymphocytes (LGL), T cells that are wreaking havoc, and a lot of rogue antibodies that are attacking his immune system. He has a high white blood count, high liver enzymes, low platelets and high clotting factors. Still there's no evidence of cancer, which is good news, but he is sick and needs to be treated.
    Last week, David Miklos said these were "weird labs." His best guess is that Barry is losing the graft. He described what is going on in Barry's immune system as a civil war between the graft and the host. It's Gettysburg, three years in. Julia doesn't like this analogy. She thinks it makes Barry the South. But I'm thinking North and most of us know who ultimately won. (When I say, "most of us," I am thinking of my close friend Ann, whose mother always told her the South actually won. As I see how things are playing out, she may have been right.)

David has conferred with his mentor at Harvard, who is a big macher at the American Society for Blood and Marrow Transplantation, and told us Barry was the subject of part of the Stanford BMT Retreat today. We're being treated by the best and the brightest and that gives us much comfort, but what he has is also very unusual. According to David, there's no data, no literature, no studies, nada. They've "never seen this before."

Barry will go into the hospital tomorrow for three or four days of treatment with ATG—a monoclonal antibody he was treated with prior to his transplant three years ago—that will kill the rogue T cells. It's nasty stuff but will hopefully do the job. They will be monitoring his counts to make sure the treatment is effective. He will come home for about a week to let the outlaws die off and then he will be infused with his donor's frozen cells in a boost as well as a DLI (donor lymphocyte infusion). He will also be on an immunosuppressant (cyclosporine) and acyclovir to prevent a recurrence of the zoster that almost killed him in 2006. He will be immunosuppressed but will not have to be in isolation. He'll just have to be careful.

We're glad to have a plan but we're not glad to have to have a plan. It's been, to say the least, emotionally draining (hell) on both of us, and we're back in cancerland even though there's no cancer. As the famous Yankee catcher, Yogi Berra, put it, "It's deja vu all over again."

All of your cards, emails, and phone calls give us great comfort.

Much love to all,

Bonnie

* * *

BARRY:

I am only hours away from my boost when Dr. Miklos walks into my hospital room looking glum. "I've got bad news and good news," he says.

Typically for me, I ask for the bad news first. I mean, isn't a happy ending better than a bad one?

His shoulders hunch as he says: "The bad news is the boost is off. The biopsy shows you have T cell leukemia. The boost won't work on that."

We know about T cell leukemia. (In April 2006, I was mistakenly diagnosed with it because I had a population of weird T cells. The prognosis, we were told, was seven months untreated, maybe a year with treatment.)

Okay, enough with the bad news already. "So, what's the good news?" I ask.

"The good news is that they didn't just take a boost supply of stem cells from your donor. We got enough to do a whole new stem cell transplant, *enough for a complete graft. If you decide to do it, we will do a more rigorous preparation this time."*

I'm not sure I want to go through that again. First, there's that hellish prep and then another hundred days in semi-isolation. There's another chance of dying right then and there. More risk of graft versus host disease that can kill you or make the rest of your life miserable. But then I recall that week I'd just spent with my family in Palm Springs and despite the fatigue and bloodshed it was memorable; Mimi was a laugh a minute.

My daughter Julia is expecting in February. I so want to see a second grandchild. Bonnie and I have had some wonderful times over the last two years. I want more time with Bonnie, my family, and my very large village of loving and caring friends, but I can't have much of that if I am in the shape I'm currently in.

I spend a few hours thinking it over. I know that we all tend to say things when we are feeling relatively okay, that we would never want to be put through this or that; we'd want someone to pull the plug. I am feeling some of that, yet there is a big part of me that says: "Roll the dice. All you've got to lose is a couple of months and the up-side is so big." Look at it this way: you say "no" and it's over. Maybe that's the right move. You never know. I know people who've said it. "No more treatment. Let nature take its course." They've had enough. They couldn't see an upside and they were drained. I can see that point of view. I'm just not there. All you really know is that decision's irrevocable. So I decide to cast the die.

I begin my second course of Campath, the monoclonal antibody that got me into remission for my first transplant in 2006. I'd forgotten how uncomfortable it made me. Once again it knocks me out. Night times, I sweat through pajamas. Daytimes, I'm constantly freezing. My skin itches and breaks out in rashes. I develop a CMV infection and then another different infection. I am sick and exhausted a lot of the time. But slowly, my blood counts improve until finally things look like they are turning around.

* * *

BONNIE:

When we got the news that Barry needed a second transplant we were devastated, to say the least. We cried a lot. The concept of repeating the whole routine, with all of its attendant risks, fears, and horrors, was almost unfathomable. Neither of us felt we could do it again. But, what was our choice? To give up and face certain and fairly quick death, or try again? There really was no choice.

Feb. 18, 2010
Bumpy Ride Towards Second Transplant

Dear Family & Friends,
    Many of you have contacted me to ask how we are doing. It's a very long and sometimes tedious story. I will attempt to make it clear and real. What we know:
    Barry has a form of T cell Leukemia. Dr. Steven Coutre, Barry's Stanford hematologist and Director of the Hematology Clinic, describes his diagnosis as "definitely weird." He will be Barry's treating physician until we move back to David Miklos for transplant.
    You may recall Barry had a T cell problem all along, and according to David Miklos had a "messy diagnosis" from day one. This is not a transformation of his B cell leukemia or a result of his transplant but another animal altogether. The T cell leukemia basically exploded as Barry lost his first graft.
    Barry is in his fourth week of Campath, the same monoclonal antibody that got him into remission in preparation for his first transplant. We go to Stanford three times a week for a subcutaneous shot in his abdomen. He had many symptoms in the beginning of this treatment (fevers, chills, dizziness, and sleeplessness) but they have subsided. His counts (white blood, hematocrit, neutrophils, lymphocytes, platelets, etc.) are looking very good. It looks like the Campath is killing off the really bad T cells and antibodies that were attacking his platelets and we are hopeful that this treatment will bring him to remission again.
    Meanwhile, we've had two Emergency Room visits. One was minor, but the other required our first ever trip in an ambulance from the clinic waiting room at the Cancer Center to the ER as Barry was having extreme shortness of breath. We thought he was dying. About twenty-seven hours later, after heart attack and pulmonary embolism were ruled out, we went home. The next day, we found out that Barry has CMV (cytomegalovirus), a common viral infection that goes along with Campath. It was probably not the cause of the ER visit but we felt it contributed.
    We are now going to Stanford every day for an infusion of gancyclovir, a powerful anti-viral. Barry has a PICC line in his arm, so at least he doesn't have to get stuck anymore. This is an exhausting regimen and we are hoping it will end soon. We are completely burned out.
    We do not know when the second transplant will occur, or if it might even be two transplants, one autologous (from his own stem cells to further clear out the marrow) followed by an allogeneic (from his angel donor's stem cells). David Miklos had said he wanted to do it fairly

quickly, but Steven Coutre has said that Barry will be on Campath for at least six weeks and maybe up to twelve (the normal course). They will have to do a bone marrow biopsy—it will be Barry's twelfth—to determine the state of the cancer.

Wes Brown, the amazing infectious disease doc associated with the BMT/Hematology program at Stanford, is our new best friend. She knows Barry very well, as she saved his life when he had the disseminated shingles in his blood in 2006. She always remarks positively about his reserves of energy, and notes that he tolerates treatment and responds to it well. Our emotional states are up and down. We are definitely hopeful that Barry will make it to a second transplant and have more good years ahead. The thought of going through the whole shebang once again is enormously daunting, but we are prepared to do it. What other choice is there?

I have found it difficult to write or talk on the phone most days, which is why you haven't heard from me and why I rarely return phone calls or emails. Please understand, I am barely able to function some days. We are working to set up a (private) website for future communications so that I can update everyone more regularly. You will also be able to leave comments there.

We're on our way to Stanford now for a longer infusion (four hours) of IVIG (intravenous immune globulin). Since insurance takes three to five working days to approve this, we signed a waiver yesterday for $46,019.36! One might ask about the thirty-six cents, but oh well.

Love to all,
Bonnie

Mar. 27, 2010
Update Re: Barry's Health

Dear Family & Friends,

Barry just completed his eight-week course of Campath and we have a bit of a reprieve. He will have yet another bone marrow biopsy on April 12 with results (the verdict) on April 19. If he is in complete remission he will get a transplant, but we do not have any further information on when that would be. Our best guess is sometime in May. All indications of complete remission are good, but they can't really tell from his regular (peripheral) blood draws—they have to look at the marrow to have a definitive answer. If he is in partial remission, he will have further treatment with another drug, nelarabine, and we do not know how long that course of treatment could last.

Barry's feeling pretty good now but has been battling infections. We *had another ER visit last week that was really no fun at all. He had a fever and we spent twenty-one hours at the Emergency Department and got three hours of sleep. He had been diagnosed with yet another viral infection, MPV (metapneumovirus), which they were not treating because they did not feel like it was dangerous unless he got a fever or shortness of breath. Since he got the fever, he finished a course of ribavirin and he's doing much better. His cough from this virus was downright scary.*

We are both completely burned out. Barry has not been writing, although he has re-surfaced on Facebook. We are both very appreciative of the notes, emails, and phone calls that we receive from you. Please forgive me if I can't always pick up the phone or reply to emails.

After my last communication, so many of you offered to cook we have a full freezer. I will get in touch with those of you who offered when we need more. Between our travels to Stanford, my attempts to work as much as possible while I can, interfacing with all of the doctors and nurses, and the rest of the hyper-vigilant life we are leading, cooking is the last thing I can do.

The things that give us pleasure, though, are very sweet. Our new grandson, Silas, and our granddaughter, Mimi, top the list. We are going to Big Sur next weekend for a quick getaway while we can and some dear friends are bringing food for our Seder on Monday.

We are also grateful to the doctors, nurses, physician assistants, nurse practitioners and case managers at Stanford. We don't have to second-guess, get second opinions, or do our own research. Stanford does it all, including interfacing with the insurance company when there is a denial or delay in approving prescriptions or procedures. And the drive to Stanford is beautiful. It's only about thirty-five minutes on one of the most beautiful freeways in California, I-280, with no trucks and hardly ever traffic. It's much better than driving across town.

We are both also thrilled that the Health Care Bill passed. While it has some major flaws, it is a first step and could definitely even affect us, the lucky ones with insurance, with its ban on lifetime limits.

Wishing everyone a joyous Passover, a happy Easter, and a beautiful spring.

Love,
Bonnie

* * *

BARRY:

On April 12, I had yet another biopsy. The results showed I'm in remission and eligible for a second transplant. I started working out with my trainer, Angela, and have returned to yoga.

April 22, I received a report on my chimerism. The original graft is almost entirely gone. It is as if I never received a transplant in 2006.

* * *

BONNIE:

April 24, 2010
The Transplant Is On—Part Deux

Dear Family & Friends,
  David Miklos emailed us Thursday morning (6:37 a.m.) with this news:

> *Congratulations! Our pathologists do not see any PLL in the bone marrow biopsy. The key statement is: 'Flow cytometry shows a significant population of T cells with loss of CD7 expression. This population does not have the immunophenotypic characteristics of the patient's prior neoplasm.*
>
> *I am meeting with my BMT colleagues this afternoon for our weekly faculty meeting and will propose we take you to a reduced intensity conditioning allo HCT with the frozen product we have. I think we should use the Fred Hutch RIC using two hundred total body irradiation with three days of fludarabine because you never had a full engraftment the first time using TLI/ATG and we are going back with the same donor.*
>
> *We could start as soon as radiation therapy logistics allow. Paige will be in touch with you about that. Once again this is good news. Congrats. I'm happy for you.*

Medical jargon aside, this means Barry is in complete remission and will have a second transplant! We do not have a date yet, but we expect it will be in about three or four weeks, as they have begun scheduling tests that precede the transplant such as pulmonary function, ECG and a CT scan. We will once again move down to Stanford and rent an apartment for the duration—about four months—and Barry will be in isolation during that time.

The "frozen product" that David mentions are the stem cells from Jennifer, Barry's original donor, an amazing woman who has given so much. He was supposed to receive a "boost" of her cells before they discovered the new T cell leukemia in January; her donation, fortunately, was enough for a full graft. We are so grateful.

David is proposing a different conditioning system (Fred Hutch RIC from Seattle) to clear out the marrow and further depress the immune system. This combination of radiation and chemo is stronger in intensity than the Stanford conditioning that Barry had previously, as the original graft never completely took over. This transplant comes with a higher risk but it is our only hope for a cure.

Needless to say, we are experiencing the full spectrum of emotions. Happiness, fear, anticipation, hope, anxiety, anger, relief, and gratitude— you name it, we've got it. And the last few months have been a whirlwind of stress that has taken its toll. The waiting and not knowing were the most difficult.

Once again, we are fortunate to have excellent health insurance through my employer.

Your support and love keep us going.

With love and hope,

Bonnie

∗ ∗ ∗

BARRY:

On April 27, just two weeks pre-transplant, I score in the ninety-fourth percentile in a pulmonary test, where you blow into a tube, so I am still qualified as a blowhard.

On April 30, my granddaughter Mimi brings her parents for a visit and meets her new cousin, Silas. I get to see it—two grandchildren thanks to transplant number one. Even though it didn't stick, it's given me that, and I have nothing to complain about there. Whatever else may happen, my decision to try a second transplant has borne tangible rewards. I've already won the lottery.

May 14, 2010—Playing the Odds

I receive my first infusion of fludarabine, a chemo that is supposed to destroy my immune system. I'm scheduled for a hefty dose of radiation next Tuesday. I am committed.

According to Dr. Miklos, the stats say I've got a fifty-fifty chance that the disease will make a comeback. If I don't take this chance, I've got a hundred percent chance that I'll relapse. When I ponder my odds, I'm reminded of a story I heard maybe fifteen years ago about an octogenarian multimillionaire. In his late eighties, he took up with a Playboy bunny one-quarter his age. His friends all shook their heads. Rumors abounded that she was cheating on him. Finally, one of his close friends got up the courage to talk to him about it, hoping that he could bring the old fellow to his senses.

"Don't you know," his friend said to the old man, "she's going out with younger men—making a fool out of you? Everyone is laughing behind your back. For every night she spends in your bed she probably spends ten with young studs."

The old man chortled. "Of course, I know," he said. "But as a businessman I also know that ten percent of something is a lot better than a hundred percent of nothing."

That's how I feel about this ordeal I have just embarked upon. I'll keep you posted.

Transplant day, May 18, I begin with eighteen minutes of radiation. This is total body irradiation, which means I get zapped in places where, for me, the sun don't normally shine. I have to stand throughout. By minute seventeen, I am sweating as if I were in a sauna and nearly collapse. They stop the bombardment and bring me a chair and a fan so I can recover enough to stand for the last minute. Then they roll me out in a wheelchair. It is no walk in the park. That night it feels like sunburn in those especially sensitive locations—a gift that keeps on giving.

I don't remember much of the infusion. Now everyone tells me I smell like creamed corn (because of the DMSO preservative they put in with the cells). I can't smell it though. I'd like to get just one whiff to know what they are talking about. It's a little embarrassing tottering around smelling like creamed corn. They say it will go away soon. That's fortunate. I don't even like creamed corn.

There was a big up yesterday when I woke from one of my many naps. Mimi was on video chat. I sat down in front of the computer and she came running toward it, saying "Baabee" or something close. She recognized me, remembered my name and was happy to see me. It makes going through this worth it.

***

BONNIE:

May 19, 2010
Successful Transplant #2—The Long Slog Is On

Dear Family & Friends,

Yesterday Barry received the previously frozen cells from his donor via infusion. It all went very smoothly, although it was a very weird experience for both of us. The cells had been frozen in five separate bags inside flat metal disks. We had been under the impression that they had been in a freezer but we were told that they had been packed in something much stronger, liquid gas, to a temperature of minus 175 degrees. The BMT Tech wheeled in a large cart with two coolers and a warm bath on top. One bag had been defrosted and it had an expiration time of four hours post-defrost. One by one, the other bags were put in the warm bath to defrost and then infused into Barry. The four other bags had expiration times of thirty minutes. It was like a production line, with the BMT tech, the physician assistant, and the nurse all checking name, date of birth, medical record number, number on bag, donor number, etc., many, many times. They did not make any mistakes and we felt very confident. The whole transplant took about thirty-five minutes.

Barry tolerated it very well. No untoward events have occurred so far. He went into this transplant very strong and healthy, which is a good thing. And this time he WON'T get shingles, which made him so sick the last time and threatened his life as well. He is on a prophylactic dose of acyclovir, and although there are no promises, we feel like all precautions are being taken.

So now the hundred days has begun and our daily routine is set. Every morning we go to the Cancer Center where he has blood draws (through his central venous catheter) and hydration (also through his catheter); he meets with nurses to check medications and with physician assistants and doctors who examine him and answer any questions we have. The nutritionist is also around to answer any questions about the low-microbial diet he must be on. After a little while, perhaps a week or two, we will start to get days off.

The rest of our days are spent dispensing medications (Bonnie), eating (both of us), sleeping (Barry), making sure he drinks three liters/day of liquids (Bonnie), preparing meals (Bonnie), doing laundry, keeping the apartment in order and sanitary (Bonnie), taking care of family business

(Bonnie), perhaps checking into my work (Bonnie), on and on. I am trying to do the shopping and errands while Barry is at the Cancer Center, as I am not allowed to leave him alone ever. Next week I hope to start working with my trainer and doing some other things for myself while local friends come and Barry-sit.

Doing this the second time around is easier, although who needed it to be easier, or even to have it be?

We are very happy in our 820 sq. ft. apartment. It's got a lot of light and a lovely view of the hills to the West. We are also happy that we moved down here a few days early and got settled in. Many thanks to Julia for her awesome tech support. I could have done it myself, but my brain was not (is not?) functioning. We just wish it would stop raining. Enough already with the rain!

With much love,
Bonnie

* * *

BARRY:

May 20, 2010—Another Point of View

It is post-transplant, day two. I have a slight nausea and a persistent headache that is more annoying than debilitating. I am consuming about thirty pills a day and god only knows what they are doing. Don't ask me what they are. That's Bonnie's department. I drink about three liters of liquids per day and most of my drinks taste pretty crummy because of the chemical taste in my mouth. Needless to say, I'm spending a lot of time peeing and washing my hands. My skin is very sensitive.

* * *

BONNIE:

June 17, 2010
Nine Fun-Filled Days at Stanford Hospital

Dear Family and Friends,

Barry and I got back to our apartment on Tuesday after spending nine days in virtual isolation in the hospital. He had fevers, headaches, chills, sweats, intestinal problems, etc., not to mention anxiety and depression. While we may never exactly know what the diagnosis was/is, he's much better. The theory we like the best, according to the amazing Wes Brown, is that he had an underlying infection, probably sinusitis, and then had fever reactions to IV antibiotics, probably Vancomycin.

Because Barry has no immune system to speak of, any tiny infection can be very dangerous. That's why we can't see people here in Palo Alto, except for our immediate family and some very close local friends who can spell me when I need to do errands, or do something for myself. (What a concept!) Barry is only allowed to be in the apartment, in the car on the way to the hospital, the ITA, or outside taking a walk. When he is any place other than inside the apartment, inside the ITA or a hospital room, he has to wear his HEPA Filter Mask. He needs someone with him at all times. It's a very limited existence but the hope is that this will save his life.

When he was in the hospital, Barry was seen by the BMT team. For some reason Wes Brown, our go-to doc when Barry is sick, wasn't notified that Barry had been admitted and she didn't get my original voicemail message that he'd been admitted. When I called her again after four days she came right over and was completely present for us. She told us that she was looking at patterns of Barry's fevers (constantly from home) to try and figure things out. Last Sunday (!) morning I called her at 8 a.m. (I have her cell and home numbers) because Barry had a really bad night. She got to the hospital at nine (despite Stanford graduation traffic) and was very reassuring about his progress. When she left she said, "I'm so glad you called. Call me anytime."

Sunday night, the nurses from the ITA called Barry to see how he was doing and to say they were looking forward to us coming back. Since these people are our social life, it means a lot that they are so caring, not to mention extremely competent.

Today is day thirty. We are scheduled to be here for one hundred days post-transplant. Hopefully the next seventy days will be uneventful.

Thanks for all of your phone calls, emails, website comments, cards, etc. Please don't be surprised if I can't respond.

Much love,

Bonnie

* * *

BARRY:

June 18, 2010—A Stir-Crazy Nine Days

I'm baaack! Just when you thought it was safe to go on my blog and get the objective facts from Bonnie, here I am to give you the unexpurgated (Well not quite—I do expurgate a bit) version of "The Hospitalization" *starring an award winning cast, including a beleaguered, overworked twenty-four/seven caregiver, a team of MDs, nurses, and a very sick and grumpy patient.*

Saturday, June 5, I'm totally wiped. I sleep from two in the afternoon to nine the following morning and wake up un-refreshed. Bonnie calls the ITA and they tell us to come right in. Soon I have a fever. They try some Tylenol but the fever and chills keep bouncing back. After several hours, I am admitted to the hospital. I'm thinking, well maybe a day or two at the most, which shows I'm not thinking.

By Monday, I'm loaded up on a bunch of antibiotics. I'm pissing in a plastic urinal so they can measure every last drop coming out of me. I want to sleep but there's no way. The parade never ends. Six a.m. blood draws. Seven a.m. vitals. Eight a.m. a tray with something they have the effrontery to claim is breakfast. For liquids, the fare consists of tiny cans of over-sweetened fruit-flavored juices that suck all the moisture out of your mouth. During rounds, the docs hover over me, promising they'll get a handle on this. They spend forever going over the meds with the nurses and Bonnie. (She gave them all the right info on Sunday night, but the computer wouldn't accept it. The computer is frequently wrong.) I'd like to use the urinal, since they're also pumping me with fluids, but it's a bad time. Then it's time for mid-day meds and another set of vitals. Next thing I know, they're bringing in a tray with "lunch." I don't want to eat. I'm chilled. There'll be more vitals soon. Afternoon meds. Housekeeping. A visit from the dietician who wants to know whether I'm eating and pooping. (In fact everyone wants to know about poop. The whole hospital is poop crazy if you ask me. But don't ask. If you do, I'll know you're one of them.) As the clock rolls around to five or so, it's time for blood draws. Then another tray of generic "food." Evening rounds follow. Interspersed over the first several days are chest x-rays and CT scans. All the while, I'm bouncing a fever between normal and 100.8°F. I'm chilled and sweating. Have I been radiation poisoned?

But enough of the kvetching. I am privileged to have some very nice and interesting nurses. Lisa is an upbeat Irish woman married to an Iranian. They have a three-year old. Her mum still lives in Galway, I think. She reminds me of the protagonist in Brooklyn, *by Colm Toibin. When Bonnie is out of the room, she tells me, "You've got a good woman there." (I am fully aware of it.) Aracely is a middle-aged Salvadoran woman who started her medical career as a nurse's aide many years ago. In the interim, she's become an RN with a certification in oncology, which is no small task. She's living proof that the anti-immigrant yahoos are really harming this country. And then there's Brian, a Portuguese son of Fall River, MA. We spend a lot of time lamenting the psychology of buying into the Sox, Bruins, and, to a lesser extent, the Celts; how they (used to) take us to the limits, year after year, only to collapse. What can you do when you've grown up in eastern MA? As kids, we were stuck with these perennial "wait 'til next year" bums. But wait, how about those Sox and Pats?*

On Wednesday, Dr. Aaron Logan, who originally participated in diagnosing my PLL says there's a possibility that my central venous catheter may be causing my infection. He pulls it, leaving me in need of a peripheral IV. In fact, I need two IVs. The first one goes in fine, the second, not so fine. They call in the charge nurse who treats my arm like a glob of pizza dough. She crams the needle in. My arm is not happy. It protests and requires hot packs for the rest of its stay in the hospital. But fortunately I get a PICC line two days later and the IVs are history. We've been through this before.

On Thursday, Dr. Wes Brown, the maestro of infectious diseases in transplant patients, enters stage left. She changes some meds. Now I'm on antifungals and antibiotics. One of these, I'm told, causes hallucinations. I'm game—except that in the back of my mind, I've had a previous encounter with these Big Pharma hallucinogenics and recall it consisted of black spiders crawling all over the walls, ceilings and floors. Well to quote the eloquent trash talk of our former prez, "bring it on!"

Shortly after the dose, I take a walk in the corridor and to my amazement the edges of all the doors are flashing on and off with strings of Christmas lights. They're pretty, but it is nowhere near Christmas, and besides, you couldn't open or shut the doors without crushing the pretty lights. Okay, Big Pharma, is that the best you can do?

By the following Monday, my episodes of fever are diminished. I'm no longer sweating at night or chilled. The docs on the team hint that I'll be out later in the week. We start thinking Thursday or Friday. The next morning they tell me I've matriculated. Four hours later I receive my discharge papers. I vow to not go back to stir.

BONNIE:

June 27, 2010
100% Engraftment—Still a Long Ways to Go

Dear Family & Friends,
We received terrific news on Friday. We were in one of the treatment rooms. A doctor who was on the BMT team popped his head into the room and said: "Barry Willdorf—one hundred percent engrafted!" and then mentioned that prednisone might become Barry's new best friend.

(Well, if you know anything about that drug, you know it causes bad stuff too, like osteoporosis, mood swings, and diabetes, and it suppresses the immune system. Barry's relationship with prednisone will introduce us to new medical specialties.)

Barry is fully engrafted, meaning his (angel) donor's stem cells have taken over and he can now begin to recover. This is a milestone that he never reached on his first transplant and it is the reason he was given a tougher pre-transplant regimen this time. Within three minutes of getting the news, David Miklos came up to the ITA to celebrate with us, saying that maybe the fevers Barry was having were engraftment and not infection. We'll never know. There is so much of this that is a mystery to us, and unfortunately, still a mystery to the doctors as well.

So while this is wonderful news, there are many obstacles ahead of us. Barry's liver function is impaired. They have discontinued some medications to see if they could be the cause, but if it doesn't get better, he will have a liver biopsy. This could be graft vs. host disease and no one seems really freaked about it, so I will not be freaked about it.

So there's GVHD both acute and chronic to perhaps endure and hopefully successfully treat. (It can be fatal.) There's the underlying cancer that no one really believes is ever completely gone, but with a new blood supply, now can be fought. There's a fifty/fifty chance of relapse within the first year post-transplant. There's the risk of infection for a long time because immune systems don't bounce back easily—it takes one to two years and there's no test to let you know when it's functioning again.

And Barry's still feeling lousy. He's very weak, fatigued, having some intestinal problems, some low-grade fevers, headaches, and more. Yesterday we spent eight hours at the ITA while he got two units of blood. Many of you have asked what happens when we go to the ITA.

1. We wait for his appointment,
2. He gets weighed and "roomed" either in a chair in a big room with

other patients, all BMT or Hematology, or in a private room with a bed if he's feeling poorly or has an active infection,

3. *His nurse takes blood through his PICC line,*
4. *They start a liter of fluids. Barry has to have three liters/day of fluids to counteract the cyclosporine immune-suppressant he's taking and he might as well get one while we're there,*
5. *He often gets one or two bags of magnesium,*
6. *After about an hour we get the blood results, CBC, differential (BMT) and chemistries and maybe some other treatments, like yesterday's red blood,*
7. *We see a PA and he gets examined,*
8. *The nurse goes over all of his medications and dosages with me,*
9. *Sometimes we see a BMT doctor, the attending, or Wes Brown comes over to examine him and chat with us.*

I read a lot while he's there, sometimes listen to music if the room is too noisy, and often take the time to go to the grocery store and do errands. I only leave if there's nothing happening, if we're not waiting to see someone, or for some significant results; if I did leave, those kinds of things would definitely occur while I'm gone and Barry would misunderstand a lot of it, forget some, and not hear the rest.

All of the doctors are very reassuring about Barry's symptoms. They keep saying: "After all you've been through, with two transplants, two courses of Campath, chemo, radiation, and whatnot, of course you feel lousy."

So is this transplant harder or easier than the last? I think harder. Even though Barry's hospitalizations haven't been life-threatening like the last time, this is the second-time around and the risks are higher. (David Miklos also said the other day that very few people get one hundred percent engraftment on a second transplant; I'm glad he didn't tell us that before.) It's completely exhausting and also a very isolating experience. We're living in a beautiful apartment complex, with nice places to walk, a pool, and a hot tub, and the weather has been glorious, as seen from our closed windows. I guess I'm sounding whiny.

In reality, we are very encouraged. While before Friday we were guardedly optimistic, now I would say that we are cautiously optimistic. Not sure if that explains it but it's the best I can do.

With much love,
Bonnie

* * *

BARRY:

July 1, 2010—The Leukemia Diet

Are you a couch potato? Have you grown too large for your Snuggy™? Do you hate to exercise and prefer cultivating bedsores? Maybe you like to eat carbs but still want to lose weight. I have just the diet for you!

You've heard about leukemia and lymphoma, I'm sure. Did you know that chemo and radiation act as a powerful ally in the fight against excess weight? They make food taste terrible. Even though the curative treatments deliver day upon day of fatigue and energy loss, why should you care? You're on the sofa anyway. You'll have enough in reserve most days to punch commands into the remote. Trust me. I've lost nearly twenty pounds in thirty days and don't have exercise to blame. So whether or not you have one of the dreaded "L"s, you might want to give a thought to a strong dose of radiation, chemo, and associated pills. Get on that couch and lose those unsightly pounds!

Small print disclaimer: Side effects may include nausea, diarrhea, constipation, shortness of breath, swollen ankles, edema in the lungs, headaches, renal failure, liver failure, heart failure, strokes, and death. But what the hell, you're well on your way with that stuff already. The thing you don't want to happen is for side effects to become the main act.

July 1, 2010—So, You Think You've Got Problems

On Friday night, my PICC line got clogged. We had to go to the hospital as the Cancer Center was closed. The nurses said I needed a clog-busting enzyme to Roto-Rooter it out. While Bonnie and I were waiting for the doctor's orders to inject the enzyme, a young Hispanic man shuffled wearily into the waiting area and slumped into a chair.

The three of us began talking. His wife—thirty years old—had just been hospitalized. He told us she had aplastic anemia, which meant she's producing no red blood, no white blood and no platelets. They have two children, three and one. Six months after the birth of their second child, she went back to work but was very tired and bruised easily. After a few days, her supervisor told her to see a doctor. That's when it was discovered.

She was about to undergo a transplant when she developed appendicitis. Given her blood counts, they couldn't operate. Her appendix burst. It seemed hopeless. As a last resort they pumped her full of antibiotics. To their amazement, the antibiotics dried up the infection and miraculously, she was saved. But that was just their first hurdle. Next came the transplant. On the day before, the couple married.

Her transplant failed to fully engraft. A boost failed to correct the downward track. And now, exactly a year later, they were back fighting for her life. As we spoke, they were pumping her full of blood products in hope that they could perform a second transplant and another miracle.

Later, we related this story to one of the nurses in the ITA. She said they were seeing a lot of young mothers who had developed a blood cancer shortly after giving birth. She speculated that it was hormonally induced. I'm sixty-five. My kids are grown and I got to watch them all the way. My heart goes out to that beleaguered family.

* * *

BONNIE:

July 26, 2010
Five Years, But Who's Counting?

Dear Family & Friends,

It is five years from the date of Barry's diagnosis of CLL (chronic lymphocytic leukemia). The good news is that he's still here, feeling good and looking good. The bad news is that we're still dealing with this shit.

Last Monday, we got the results of the second chimerism (engraftment) test and the engraftment had gone down. Needless to say, we were very upset, as were the docs, especially since Barry lost the first graft, which led to a nastier and more aggressive cancer.

What the doctors think has happened is that—either because of the CMV (cytomegalovirus), a common infection for immune-compromised people which he contracted soon after the first chimerism test, or because of the ganciclovir which treats the CMV—the graft has been impacted. Right in the middle of the first transplant Barry had the terrible zoster infection. Now Dr. Miklos thinks that might have affected the first transplant. The ganciclovir depresses the white blood count and the marrow, so that might be another factor in the current graft loss.

Last week's CMV level went way down. (They test every Monday with results on Wednesday or Thursday.) Everyone's very happy about that. They're doing several things to attack this problem and hopefully the engraftment will go back up. Apparently this can happen.

Barry's been switched from ganciclovir to foscarnet, another anti-viral which does not depress the white blood count, but is really hard on the kidneys. He's getting IVIG infusions (immunoglobulin which fights infection) once a week. If his white blood count does not recover on its own, he will get shots of Neupogen.

Today is day sixty-eight and the next chimerism test will be on day ninety, with results about a week later. Waiting, waiting, waiting. Breathing a lot.

When discussing Barry's meds and his viruses, Dr. Benjamin, the attending in the ITA this month, says, "we're threading a needle." Obviously there are no guarantees but there's a plan based on a set of hypotheses. So we are hoping for the best.

Our life here in Palo Alto has improved. The stir-crazy, fresh-air deprived days are hopefully over. Since Barry is feeling so much better and is also stronger, we are going for long walks and having outdoor visits from family and friends. They lift our spirits. We also sit by the pool and read. We've both been reading a lot and watching many movies. I'm finally able to work out regularly with my wonderful trainer, Angela. Visits from our children and grandchildren, and photos/videos sent regularly and posted to their blogs bring us great joy.

For those of you who are looking for Barry's postings on his blog, do not feel deprived. While he has not been writing too much about the transplant experience, he has been finishing the final edits on his book, "Flight of the Sorceress," which will be published as an e-book, perhaps as early as September. We'll keep you posted.

As always, your emails, cards, phone calls, and comments on the Web site are welcome and incredibly meaningful to us.

With much love and quite a bit of hope,

Bonnie

* * *

BARRY:

August 5, 2010—Around the Corner: Eighty Days

As the apocalyptics say: "The end is near." It's getting close. Tomorrow will be eighty days since my second transplant! We will soon go home. Bonnie is feeling like a prisoner. She gets to visit her friends every two weeks or so. When that happens, I get a visit from Sam, who cooks up something good and we get a little time to talk and watch sports.

I haven't felt much like writing since I got the news that I no longer was one hundred percent engrafted. I've been there before and the end game is no fun. I am doing everything they tell me to do—especially downing three liters of liquids every day. Every other day, I get to see new blood counts. I hang on the results. Right now things seem to be holding, but I am looking for improvement, so I'm not getting what I want and growing a bit whiny.

In any event we will get to go home in about three weeks and I am looking forward to better dining options and getting to see more people—maybe even the opportunity to tickle a grandchild.

About two weeks ago we saw the Hispanic couple, the young mom with aplastic anemia. She was in a wheelchair. We haven't seen them again and can't ask anyone because of medical privacy issues. We hope they are okay. Knowing they were able to keep her alive as long as they have, though, was an up.

I'm not in a humorous mood because I have a bone marrow biopsy in eleven days and I always get nervous before that happens—as well as afterward, as I wait for results. That's one of the things about cancer. There's always a test on the horizon or results around the corner and you just know that it's a game of Russian roulette. One day the bullet will be lined up and boom, you're terminal. Meanwhile you bide your time waiting for a miracle cure and dealing with stress and anxiety.

* * *

BONNIE:

August 5, 2010
Interim Update—We're Going Home

Dear Family and Friends,

Yesterday we got confirmation that we can move back home the weekend of August 21/22, just a few days shy of one hundred days post-transplant. We'd been asking about this for a while, but they didn't want to give us the okay until Barry's CMV was undetectable for two weeks, which it now is, and his counts (white blood and platelets) started recovering, which they have.

Last week Dr. Miklos stopped by when we were in the ITA. I asked him whether there was any significance to the fact that the same day they did the chimerism (engraftment) test was the same day his CMV was really high. He said, "Well, think about it. Who is CMV positive?" That would be Barry as his donor is CMV negative. So Barry's T cells (T cells fight infection) were mobilized to fight the CMV and once the CMV is gone, her T cells can take over." He was very upbeat and we've been feeling that way as well.

We are very much looking forward to ending our incarceration, even though it is a lovely apartment. Being able to have fresh air and normal contact with our family and friends will be such a treat. Barry will still be on many restrictions, although he will not have to wear his HEPA filter mask except when in medical facilities. It won't be until next May that he will be able to get on an airplane, take public transportation, hug friends, and go to public events such as theater and movies or a ball game. But we will have major portions of our life back. I will return to work after Labor Day and we will not be spending twenty-four/seven together. Not that that's been a problem at all, but we are really starved for the company of others (that would be all of you).

I will keep you posted. Barry will have bone marrow biopsy number thirteen on August 16 and we will get results (chimerism and cancer) about a week later.

Much love,
Bonnie

Cross Country Road Trip — Before and After

CHAPTER TEN

Another Rollercoaster Ride

BONNIE:

September 2, 2010
News

Dear Family & Friends,
We're home—very grateful to be here and beginning slowly to recover our strength. Both of us are utterly exhausted as well as traumatized by the whole experience, which was much harder the second time around.
Barry's bone marrow biopsy of August 16 showed no evidence of disease! When we met with David Miklos on August 20, he was thrilled at the results. He said, "The cellularity is great...This marker is great..."This is as good as it gets..." and "Go live your life." He told us we didn't need to see him for three weeks and the less we see doctors the better.
Then, last night, we got the chimerism (engraftment) results. David wrote:

> *Barry and Bonnie, unfortunately, your donor chimerism is decreasing. We will recheck in thirty days as we decrease Barry's immune suppression. We will plan for DLI at six months if there is evidence of disease . . . I wish we had full donor chimerism.*
> *David*

So here we are again. Barry feels and looks great. So far, there's no evidence of disease, but as all of you cancer patients out there know, they never get every last cell; there is always a sword pointed at your head, and with decreasing chimerism the chances for relapse are magnified. We will try to breathe and stay grateful for what we have now.
We just got off the phone with David who further explained his thinking. What he is looking for is an "immune response" which will allow the

donor's cells to bounce back and take over. It is not impossible, but if that does happen, in a few months, and if there is disease progression, he will think about a DLI or treatment with chemotherapy drugs. Treating any of this now would be highly dangerous.

Talking about serious GVHD, which can be seriously debilitating as well as potentially fatal, he said, "You sat next to some of those people." He reminded us that Barry got three good years out of the last transplant, which we are always aware of, and forever grateful. We can never know what the future will bring.

And now for something completely different (which I wrote before we got the chimerism results).

Do you remember Dr. Miklos's Ten Commandments that Barry wrote about on his blog a couple of years ago?

1. *Thou shalt not enter among crowds, be they in the theater, at the movies, or in games of sport,*
2. *Thou shalt eschew public transportation, yea verily even unto BART,*
3. *Thou shalt not touch, even with thine hands, the person of another,*
4. *Thou shalt not swim or douse thy self in the waters of a hot tub,*
5. *Thou shalt not eat fish or meat that has not been overcooked,*
6. *Thou shalt avoid grasping shopping carts and all manner of like implements,*
7. *Thou shalt not imbibe of spirits even unto the fruit of the vine,*
8. *Thou shalt not fly in airplanes,*
9. *Thou shalt absent thy self from houses of worship yea even unto the High Holy Days,*
10. *Thou shalt not whine over the foregoing, but be grateful that there are not twenty such Commandments.*

Last year, at the annual BMT reunion at Stanford, another of David's patients who had happened upon it presented it as a plaque to David and he has hung it in his office. When we asked him a couple of weeks ago about some restrictions, he just said, "Consult my Ten Commandments."

So, we're back in circulation. Ready for visits, restaurants (not super crowded ones) and matinee movies. We really want to see our family and friends. We've returned to our amazing Saturday yoga class and have resumed working out with our trainer. Barry's getting regular massages, and we're making some extremely short-term plans. I'm returning to work on Tuesday.

We live with the knowledge that if Barry did not have treatment and the transplant he would not be with us now. In January, when the diagnosis of the aggressive T-cell leukemia was made, David told us that Barry could expect to live four to six months without treatment. We've beaten that already!

We are so grateful to everyone for their love and support and, of course, the incredible BMT staff at Stanford for their caring and competence. And also to my work, for the great health plan they provide and for their understanding and support during this more than stressful time.

With love, gratitude, and not a little trepidation,
Bonnie

November 3, 2010
What a week—The Good (really, really good), The Great (Giants win the Series for the first time in SF), and the Ugly (except for our fair state)

Dear Family & Friends,

What a wild ride we've been on health-wise. Last time I wrote, Barry's engraftment was dropping. Last week his white blood count and absolute neutrophil count (neutrophils fight infection) plummeted and he wasn't feeling well. After four shots of Neupogen his counts recovered and in the meantime, they did another chimerism (engraftment) test. Every single line that they test (T cells, B cells, blah blah blah) went up and three were in the 90s. We're thrilled and David Miklos is very encouraged. He thinks this happened because Barry is off all immunosuppression drugs (as well as most other drugs.)

Barry has a biopsy on November 12 and we'll talk about the results with David on November 19. When we were in the Cancer Center on Saturday, the doctor on duty asked Barry how he was doing with this rollercoaster ride. Barry said he was getting bored. I would dispute that. I'm definitely not bored. Anyway, he said that Barry is really a challenging case and that David is following every little thing and working really hard on Barry's "situation."

We weren't supposed to get the chimerism results until Monday, but Dr. Benjamin called late Saturday afternoon with the results—nearly full engraftment—and asked if Barry was still bored. Best phone call ever.

We really have been trying to live our lives somewhat normally. I'm finding that extremely difficult. I've announced my retirement as of January 6 and am really looking forward to having time without the pressure of work. I need it as I'm completely depleted.

Barry's been writing and publishing, and is on a roll.
Much love to all,
Bonnie
P.S.—so we beat Texas twice, first the Rangers, and then Prop 23. Go
California!!

* * *

BARRY:

It's winter, 2010, nearly four months after my return from Stanford. I feel like I've been in a barroom brawl.

You may be surprised to learn that once, in my youth, I actually was in a real barroom brawl, of the John Wayne variety. It happened in Torquay, England. A woman I didn't know came up to my table and sat down. She began talking. A moment later a bouncer showed up and told her to leave. She looked a little raggedy and resisted. He got rough. I told him to hold on, I'd just finish my beer and walk her outside. I picked up my glass to drain it and he knocked it out of my hand. I got up, totally surprised, and a fellow behind me hit me over the head with a chair, knocking me down. Then the two of them began kicking me. The cops came eventually and told me that it was all my fault. It was a crooked town and the thugs they called bouncers were protected.

Cancer is like those Torquay thugs. There's no fair play. Cancer sneaks up behind you and hits you over the head with a chair. Then some people tell you it's your fault.

One of the things you're going to find, if you are diagnosed with cancer, is a tendency for people to look for causes based upon your behavior. Some people, like Bill Maher, think that you can avoid cancer through diet. Others will tell you the magic bullet is exercise. Another bunch will want you to adjust your karma. People want to believe that you get cancer because you somehow violated obvious rules of behavior that, if they are scrupulously followed, will shield them from a similar fate.

Whatever their *shtick*, the presently healthy take comfort in the belief that if they keep on doing what they're doing it won't happen to them. They are wrong. Cancer can get vegans and vegetarians. It can hit the most adept yogi. Good people can get cancer. Bad people can escape it. To blame the victim is both a conceit and a defense. The more one blames, the more it evidences fear. If you are among those with a cancer diagnosis, keep this in mind. Don't blame yourself and don't accept blame from others. And if you are among the blamers, well you may just get the surprise of your life.

* * *

BONNIE:

November 20, 2010
Much to Be Thankful For

Dear Family & Friends,
   This has been a great week. Results from last week's biopsy show no disease and that Barry is almost completely engrafted. There is some evidence of graft vs. host disease beginning (taste buds not doing well, especially with sweets—oh no!), so David put Barry back on an immune-suppressive for a period of time. The good news about GVHD is that there's a graft!
   We want to wish everyone a joyous Thanksgiving. We are grateful for all of your love and support.
   Much love,
   Bonnie

* * *

BARRY:

So, I am in Dr. Miklos's Friday afternoon clinic. He's running late, as usual. This is not a bad thing. David spends all the time needed with his patients. He gives them one hundred percent attention for as long as necessary and doesn't hurry us off because he's running late. When my turn comes, we're in no rush.

He looks at my numbers. He pumps the sanitizer and rubs the goop around on his hands. Tells me to lift up my shirt so he can examine my back and neck. As he does this, he mutters a few indecipherable comments to his colleague Aaron Logan. "You've got some graft versus host," he announces in a voice that seems to me a bit giddy.

"So?"

"Well you can't have graft versus host disease unless you're engrafted," he says with a grin. "You're engrafted."

I've waited a long time to hear that, but no gift comes without a back-end price tag. What's the deal with graft versus host; I am more interested in knowing now that it is no longer hypothetical. Aaron Logan explains that it can affect a lot of organs, especially the skin, respiratory system, digestive system, and bones. It can make you go stiff. Make it difficult to breathe. If it gets really bad, it can kill you. I've been going through all of this to acquire a new disease that can kill me? Such a deal!

"We're going to put you on prednisone," Dr. Miklos says.

Well, I'd been on prednisone in 2006, just before I switched doctors and I didn't like it. Also, it didn't like me. I could feel my blood boiling whenever there was the slightest reason to anger. I'd get pugnacious and believe I could rip someone's head off. I was delusional because I believed I had the power to rip someone's head off. Probably, I'd try, and end up falling on my face like a pathetic drunk.

In the late Fall, PTSD got to Bonnie and she decided to retire from her job as regional librarian for the engineering firm of Simpson, Gumpertz and Heger. We made a decision to go on COBRA because, overall, we liked the treatment we'd been receiving from our insurer and didn't want to jump ship in the middle of the ocean. It turned out to be a huge mistake, as we would learn too late.

Buried in government small print is a rule that COBRA is not considered an employee-provided health insurance program and thus, if I failed to enroll in Medicare, Part B within eight months of her retirement, I would be subject to a ten percent penalty by Medicare for the rest of my life. Naturally, I failed to enroll in time, but I hope I end up paying that penalty for many years to come.

It came to pass that in February 2011, I embarked upon my prednisone odyssey—forty milligrams per day. It wasn't pretty. The drug unleashed anger that I didn't think I possessed. Bonnie just kept saying, "But you don't have cancer." Somehow it didn't help. We settled in, and I bided my time as the doctors managed the prednisone, bringing it down in increments.

* * *

BONNIE:

May 18, 2011
Barry's New First Birthday

Dear Friends and Family,

Today is the first anniversary of Barry's second transplant. Many people count that date as another birth date. Barry's health is good. He has some minor GVHD but that is a good thing because he has a graft. He never fully engrafted with the first transplant. He is on steroids (not a lot of fun) but we are hoping that he will be able to get off of them in the near future.

We met his amazing and generous (two-time) donor. Here's a photo of them together, taken a few weeks ago:

I found that I just couldn't work anymore, at least up to my standards, and retired in January. SGH threw me a very moving party. I will miss them. Now we are enjoying life together, especially getting immense joy from our grandchildren. At the same time, we are in deep mourning for our dear young friend, Hope Reichbach, who died suddenly at the age of twenty-two. She'd been called a "rising star" in the Brooklyn political scene and her loss will resonate.

Barry will have two books coming out in print in the next few months, "Flight of the Sorceress" and "The Fourth Conspirator," and we are still waiting for the next appeal to be denied in his case against the Oakland landlord.

Since Barry is not allowed to fly because of the danger of infection and we are anxious to get out of Dodge, we are planning a cross-country road trip this summer. We hope to see many of you along the way.

With much love and gratitude,

Bonnie

* * *

BARRY:

In late July we embarked on a seven-week cross-country road trip in a brand new Prius. America sprawled before us. We visited family and friends from Oregon to Massachusetts and back. We caught the motorcycle rally in Sturgis SD, explored the Black Hills and ferried across Lake Michigan. We brought an earthquake to DC as a present from California and in return we were treated to a hurricane. We attended our last Montana yoga retreat, ate crabs in Maryland and lobsters in Massachusetts. We saw about seventeen new babies.

* * *

BONNIE:

November 6, 2011
Update—All Good

Dear Family & Friends,
It is almost eighteen months since Barry's second transplant and he is cancer-free. (He'd rather I write, "The doctors believe he is cancer-free") The reason the docs know this is that he has chronic GVHD. There would be no GVHD without a G. It manifests itself in his skin, which is red and sclerotic, and he's being treated for this with the dreaded prednisone, a miracle drug, with very nasty emotional and physical side effects. They are finally, after much begging, tapering down on the prednisone and Barry will start in a clinical trial with nilotinib to treat the GVHD. (nilotinib is Gleevec 2.0 because Gleevec is out of patent—don't we love the drug companies . . .)
Barry asked the other day why GVHD is such a big deal if he doesn't really mind the skin problems. It was explained to us that if GVHD is not treated early, when it advances, it gets very ugly (I'll spare you the details) and has to be treated with massive doses of immunosuppressants. Then Barry would be susceptible to opportunistic infections that could be fatal. That did it for us. We're with the program.
David also gave Barry the okay to travel and swim, with his usual "You have to live your life" advice. Despite having taken our amazing seven-and-a-half-week, cross-country road trip this summer, we're raring to go and will be planning some trips for 2012 soon.
In other good news, the US Supreme Court decided not to hear the appeal that the landlord filed. Even these Supremes didn't want to touch

this guy. Game over. He has started to pay on the judgment and Barry is rightfully very proud of his team's work on this case. He took the case in February 2003 and tried it in October–November 2008. Now he's finally getting paid and the recognition he deserves. The class members are very happy. There were many times we thought Barry wouldn't live to see this day.

And finally, Barry has two books in print, The Flight of the Sorceress, *his historical novel (http://flightofthesorceress.blogspot.com/) and Burning Questions, the first part of his 1970s trilogy set in Gloucester, MA (http://1970strilogy.blogspot.com/). For those of you in the Bay Area, he will be reading from* The Flight of the Sorceress *next Sunday, November 13 at Bird & Beckett Bookstore (653 Chenery) at 3:00 pm. If you need a break from Occupying, come on by.*

Best wishes to all for a healthy and happy holiday season.
Much love,
Bonnie

* * *

BARRY:

In December, Noa, a precious little girl, was born in Brooklyn to my daughter Nina and her husband Michael. I now have lived to see three grandchildren. Everything I have gone through was worth it just for that opportunity.

I've been on prednisone for more than a year now. I started with a forty milligram per day dose. Dr. Miklos has tapered me down a number of times and I'm now at fifteen milligrams per day. I think I'm doing okay at this dose. Bonnie doesn't. She thinks I am surly and can get pretty mean.

Prednisone makes me easy to anger, I admit. But I'm not always angry. Not the whole time I'm on it anyway. I can go along pretty mellow, but when something gets my goat and I'd ordinarily get angry anyway, even if I wasn't dosed-up on that steroid, it kicks in. Kind of like a turbo-charge. Where ordinarily I'd floor it and the car would just accelerate steadily, instead I get this extra kick and then I'm in hyperspace anger. But it gets worse than that, because I'm also delusional. I think I'm capable of ripping the trunk off an elephant. Then I try to do something physical only to find I'm totally spazz. Falling down like a drunk—and maybe that's what I am—drunk on legal pills.

I point out the "legal" part just so you can be sure I'm not implying that there's any fun involved. It wouldn't be legal if it had fun attached, even fun as a remote and insubstantial byproduct of its true purpose—to get you hooked on whatever drug companies sell and doctors prescribe.

I had a conversation with a doctor while I was on prednisone. "Know what the difference is between a journeyman author and a master novelist?" I asked him.

"You tell me," he said.

"The journeyman author makes a point well and you know it. The master makes a point well and you don't even know that it's been made. The master lets you believe you thought it up all by yourself."

"Same for surgeons," he said. "A good surgeon will cut you, sew you up and get you back to normal, and you know that's what he's done because you feel it every step of the way. A great surgeon will get you back on your feet, yet you'll have no idea what a masterful job he's done for you because a lot of it, you won't even notice."

"You think? A great surgeon can do painless surgery? Is that what you are saying?"

"Well, maybe not painless but you'll heal faster. Whatever greatness it may be, it comes when you can make it look easy."

"Right now, I'm great at getting angry," I told him. "I'm really getting it down. So make whatever you're doing look real easy. Don't cross me."

"That doesn't count," he said. You're on steroids. That disqualifies you from the anger events. No Olympics for you."

I bruise easily on prednisone. I look at my arms and find big red blotches or streaks up and down my forearms. I have no idea how these things occur. I can't recall any collisions, bumps or scrapes. They seem to come easily but take a month to clear up.

My dear friend Ann just died after seventeen years of living with ovarian cancer. She was in remission for fourteen of those years. She saw her two sons grow up and become fine men. Bonnie and I saw her for the last time only two weeks before she died. She knew she was a goner. She was tired. But she still had her beautiful smile and I can still hear her voice. It's hard to believe she's dead. She was so much alive when I was close to death. This keeps happening.

* * *

BONNIE:

Prednisone is a miracle drug and a marriage destroyer. After Barry got diagnosed and we embarked upon this frightening and life-changing "journey" (I really hate that term but will use it here), we basically stopped fighting. We even stopped bickering. Except for when he was on high doses of prednisone. I remember one particular incident when I was driving, and he became enraged at another driver and flipped him off. I was really angry. He was putting us in danger and it wasn't his place to interact with the other driver. It was mine and I try not to incite road rage or violence. The other driver could have a gun. We actually brought that incident to our therapist and, since I was doing most of the driving when he was sick, he did try and not react, but it didn't always work. Sometimes the prednisone won.

* * *

BARRY:

March 30, 2012:

Aaron Logan just told me that they have been able to clone my original CLL and they can find no trace of it in my blood. He and David Miklos agree that if the second leukemia that I got was going to make a comeback, they would have detected evidence of it by now. I'd like to say I'm relieved, but I don't want to go down that road. I'm very superstitious that the minute I let my anxiety guard down, the cancer will ambush me. So no way am I about to celebrate their prognosis.

I have some GVHD symptoms despite the prednisone therapy. I have some stuff in my mouth, white patches. My GVHD is now described as chronic. Dr. Miklos wants to put me on a trial for nilotinib. The side effects are daunting. I won't begin to list them all. But the worst part for me is that I will have to give up grapefruit and grapefruit juice. Well at least that's my judgment of the worst part before I begin the trial. I may have different complaints once I confront the side effects. I begin this new odyssey on April 17, 2012. Nearly seven years after my original diagnosis.

My all-time favorite novel, *All Quiet On the Western Front*, by Erich Maria Remarque, tells the story of Paul Bauer, a young German who, just out of school, enlists in the army during the first days of World War I. He witnesses every one of his classmates either get killed or horribly wounded. He becomes the last survivor and makes it to within weeks of the end of the war, succumbing as he grasps for beauty despite his knowledge of the danger. He knows that the world as it will be after the war will be an uncomfortable place for the likes of him. War has ruined him even if it has not killed him, and so why not just get it over with? So he reaches for a butterfly in an act of suicide. Since I was diagnosed, I have survived cancer while many friends have perished. I am beginning to feel like Paul Bauer. I am willing to reach for butterflies and, remarkably, I am able to grasp them, so far, without getting shot.

* * *

BONNIE:

2012 starts out both wonderfully and terribly. Our newest granddaughter, Noa Bess was born at the end of 2011 and we go to New York to celebrate her Baby Naming Ceremony. While there we spend time with our dear friends, Gus and Ellen who lost their dear daughter, Hope, the previous Spring. Gus's pancreatic cancer is acting up again. In February we take a long-anticipated vacation to Hawaii where Barry ends up in the Molokai General Hospital (6 beds) with a nasty upper respiratory infection. So much for vacation. I go to New York by myself several times to help Nina with the girls, but everyone thinks it best for Barry not to travel, especially now that he is on the nilotinib study.

CHAPTER ELEVEN

Whack-a-Mole

BONNIE:

May 18, 2012
Two Years Today Since Transplant 2.0

Dear Family and Friends,
Today is the second anniversary of Barry's second transplant.
We met with David Miklos yesterday and I asked if Barry was "cured."
Barry was not happy about this question. He said it was a jinx.
First David said, jokingly, "I always consider my patients cured un-
til they're not." He then amended his sarcastic statement with this very
meaningful one.
"Given the nature of Barry's second cancer, T-PLL (T-cell prolympho-
cytic leukemia), an extremely rare, aggressive and deadly leukemia, he's
probably cured. He has no evidence of disease (NED) and is definitely in
remission."
David has also reminded us that this second transplant was particu-
larly risky as it was a second transplant along with the miserable cancer
it was treating.
Without this transplant, Barry had five to seven months to live, and
we've learned the success rate of transplants for T-PLL is horribly low. We
don't even know whether any of the T-PLL transplants have been a second
transplant. So the whole ordeal we went through was even riskier than we
imagined. We are very grateful.
Barry is still struggling with chronic GVHD, which manifests itself in
his skin, but is not bothersome. He is still on prednisone but the clinical
trial he began in April hopefully will get him off. He seems to be respond-
ing and yesterday David further reduced his prednisone. We both will be
very happy if he can get down to either a teeny-tiny dose or completely

get off of it. The side effects of the prednisone are difficult, including for Barry the inability for him to get rid of some terrible warts because of its immunosuppresant qualities.

In other news, we are devastated by all of our close friends struggling with cancer and mourn the loss of those who have recently passed. If you haven't seen this, yesterday's New York Times published an eloquent op-ed by our dear friend, Gus Reichbach, who is suffering from pancreatic cancer. http://www.nytimes.com/2012/05/17/opinion/a-judges-plea-for-medical-marijuana.html

On a happy note, we had a wonderful visit from our Brooklyn family in April and Barry made a lovely 3+ minute video of our three (soon to be four) grandchildren.

Hope everyone has a lovely summer.

Much love,

Bonnie

* * *

BONNIE:

July 18, 2012

Lots of News, Some Wonderful, Some Not So Wonderful

Dear Family and Friends,

The wonderful news first—we have a new grandson, Lorenzo Hector Campins—born July 5. His first name is inspired by an ancestor who was the founder of modern medicine in Venezuela. His middle name is after our dear young friend, Hope, who died last year and was like a sister to our daughters.

The terrible news is that Hope's father, Gus Reichbach, died last Saturday, of pancreatic cancer. His obit, as yet unpublished is here: http://www.nytimes.com/2012/07/19/nyregion/gustin-reichbach-judge-with-a-radical-history-dies-at-65.html. Gus and Barry and I went back a long way and shared many significant life experiences. We all first met at Columbia where Barry and Gus were in law school together. Our families traveled together, our children had a second home at Gus and Ellen's house in Brooklyn when they were in college, and their daughter, Hope, was like their little sister. He was a force of nature and will be missed by all.

In more cancer news, Barry's nasty T cells are acting up again. He has a lesion, which when biopsied, turned up a clonal population (cancer) of T cells similar to his T-PLL (T-cell prolymphocytic leukemia) that was successfully treated with a stem cell transplant in May 2010. Dr. Miklos (as well as many other doctors we have consulted with) have never seen anything like this before. We're not happy to be a unique case. The bad news is that his cancer is back. The good news is that it's localized. It's not in the bone marrow, and there are no other sites that showed up on a PET-CT scan last week. It's been described as "superficial with SUV of 6 (not very hot, suggests slow proliferation. Not too aggressive)." And it's treatable with radiation.

We don't know what an SUV is but we don't like them. We drive a Prius. David told us that sometimes rogue cancer cells hang out in the skin or in the brain. I guess we're really glad that it's not in the brain, although when we got the results of the PET-CT it showed nothing in the brain and Barry remarked that he wasn't surprised because there was nothing up there anyway.

So now we're with the Cutaneous Lymphoma group. Who ever heard of cutaneous lymphoma? But the radiation oncologist who is treating Barry (Dr. Million—we like her name) said it's not necessarily a lymphoma. Once again, a messy diagnosis. Of course we don't really care what it's called as long as they can make it go away. And we're very grateful to be at Stanford. Our favorite nurse calls David Miklos "Einstein."

Barry will get 20 days of radiation, starting very soon. It's Monday through Friday. We will still be able to go to our Offner family reunion in Milwaukee but will have to cancel our vacation (yet another vacation cancelled) planned for after that.

For those of you who know my back saga (herniated disc/caudal epidural) I am slowly improving. Hopefully no surgery in my future. While the surgery is pretty minor, it's the long recuperation that freaks me out. Especially with everything else that's going on.

Very emotional times.

Much love to all,

Bonnie

* * *

BONNIE:

Oct. 7, 2012

Barry is experiencing severe abdominal pain and bloating. After several weeks of being told it is probably a viral infection, he is scheduled to see a GI specialist and have a colonoscopy. He is in such distress when he sees the doc that they change the colonoscopy to an endoscopy, where they see nothing. He has a CT-scan later that day and is admitted to the hospital overnight because of a loss of oxygenation. He is scheduled for a paracentesis (draining of the ascites fluid from his abdomen) for the following Tuesday and is able to participate in a reading at our local bookstore, which he had organized as part of Litquake on that Sunday. I wrote the following to my children and closest friends and family:

> *David Miklos just came by. He thinks that what happened today (oxygen loss/slight fever) was an allergic reaction to the contrast liquid that Dad was given for the CT scan. Hopefully, if the night goes well, Dad will get discharged in the morning. All of those symptoms have cleared up.*
>
> *In terms of the bigger problem, the abdominal distress, they saw a lot of fluid in the abdomen (ascites), which would explain the bloating and pain. David thinks that it is a relapse of the T-cell cancer and is treatable with chemo (Nelarabine) and then the donor immune system will be able to re-activate.*
>
> *On Monday, Dad will have some fluid taken out and they'll put it through tests to see if the cancer cells are there.*
>
> *He also doesn't see the need for a colonoscopy.*
>
> *I was about to go home when David stopped by. I told him I thought he'd be home with his kids. He said that he's a bad father but a good doctor. Dad's in a double room w/no roommate and David said I could use the other bed. I love this man.*
>
> *We'll talk tomorrow.*

Monday we return to the ITA and he is again hospitalized because the pain is so severe. Tuesday he has the paracentesis and the results are ominous. T-PLL has returned. A bone marrow biopsy confines it to the abdominal area, not the marrow, but this is terrible and frightening news. To make it worse, he is taken off of the BMT service (David Miklos) and put back in Hematology where the docs are good, but just not as caring and communicative.

Here's another email to my children and closest family and friends.

> *I made it happen. Pharmacist said she couldn't get Nelarabine until Tuesday (!!!). She had called 2 local hospitals. I asked her if she'd called San Diego, City of Hope, etc. She said, "I can't call everywhere." Two hours later she came by and told us she'd located it at Oakland Childrens' Hospital and it was being taxied over. I hate it when people don't do their jobs. David stopped by last night. Was encouraging and very glad that Dad is starting chemo today. I said to him that it was very strange that Dad's blood work has been completely normal. He said that everything about*

Dad has been strange—2 transplants, cancer relapse after 2 years. He also said that "cancer is smart, but we're hoping that he is smarter."

October 12, 2012
Bad News: Cancer Relapse

Dear Family and Friends,
    Shortly after Labor Day, Barry started experiencing abdominal pain and distress. Earlier this week, after some definitive tests, we were told that his second cancer, T-cell prolymphocytic leukemia (PLL), a very rare and very aggressive cancer, is back. So after seven years, two transplants and two years, here we are again.
    We are at Stanford Hospital now and he is about to receive his first dose of nelarabine, which we hope will attack this nasty disease. We have great faith in Barry's team here.
    Below is a photo taken last Sunday at Bird & Beckett, our local bookstore, where Barry and other Sixties radicals read at a Litquake event organized by Barry. It was very successful. Unfortunately, he will be unable to read at the Litcrawl tomorrow night as scheduled. Hopefully next year.
    Much love,
    Bonnie

Photo by Maurice Kamins

* * *

BARRY:

My impressions of this October 2012 hospitalization can be summed up in four words: I want to die. I am in a great deal of pain, but I can handle that part. I have a tube in my nose that is sucking a vile liquid out of my gut that looks like Coca-Cola and smells like sewage. I can't enjoy anything and only want to sleep.

At some point I mention to Bonnie that I'd like her to slip me a whole bottle of pills that would put an end to this torment. She replies that I'm not going to die and she doesn't want to spend the rest of her life in prison. I feel betrayed. What's a caregiver for if not to meet my suicidal whims?

Somehow, a nurse manages to get wind of my desires and the next thing I know a young woman doctor pops into my room telling me she's some kind of shrink and wanting to know whether I am "thinking about hurting myself."

What kind of dumb question is that? Can't she just come out and talk straight? Are they unable to teach the words, "kill," "death," and "suicide" in med school? "Hurt myself?" I snap back. "Fuck no, I don't want to hurt myself. I hurt enough already. I want to kill myself."

Of course all hell breaks loose at that point. I have a massage sched-uled. She wants me to cancel it so she can talk me out of whatever the fuck she thinks I'm planning. I've got no gun, no poison, no drugs, no knife and there's no way you can bump yourself off by a massage. "I'm having a mas-sage in a couple minutes," I tell her. "Get the fuck out!" She doesn't want to go, but eventually my intimidating mannerisms convince her it's for her own good. I get the massage without fatal consequences. Afterward, her boss shows up and determines I'm not an imminent threat of putting the hospital at risk of liability.

A few days later, a Muslim woman drops by and asks if I want counsel-ing. "Sure, why not," I reply. We have a nice long chat. She doesn't mind if I'm Jewish just as I don't mind she's Muslim. Counseling a man does not trouble her, and I'm not bothered that she's a woman. In fact, I think we're both a little amused by the breakdowns of stereotypes. She returns a few days later and we have another nice conversation. We're not so very different, her and me.

I also get a brief visit from Dr. Miklos, who tells me I am not dying de-spite my pain, but if I want to die, I should check out of here and go home. "It will be a painful six months," he predicts, "but you'll accomplish your goal." I decide to stay put.

BONNIE:

This hospitalization is very difficult. Barry's in a lot of pain, on a lot of drugs, and is not very coherent. He wants me to kill him. I decline, telling him I don't want to go to prison. One of the docs who shall remain nameless has a terrible bedside manner. He keeps talking about "pulling the trigger on Campath" when he means that it might be time to put Barry back on Campath because the other treatments aren't working as yet. Very poor choice of words. I tell him that and he kind of laughs. Another email to my children and closest folks:

> *Dad's going to get 2 doses of Fludarabine, another chemo. (Megan mentioned this as a possibility before the docs did!). One tonight and one tomorrow. Just more ammunition to kill the cancer. He also had PT and OT today and is going down on the pain meds.*
>
> *David just stopped by. We talked about the good news (marrow clear) and the conundrum that we are presented with. There's no way to test for the cancer since they usually tell from biopsies. Dad's regular blood work has been totally normal. When Dad feels better, that will be the test.*
>
> *I said that I was happy that Dad's still here after 7 years, and David said we're going for 7 more. I'll take that.*
>
> *BTW, the nelarabine never came from the manufacturer. They had to send someone to UC Davis to get it yesterday. If I hadn't made it happen last week we'd still be waiting. David said he wants me on his team."*

Again, to our daughters, shortly after I wrote the one above:

> *Very soon after I wrote you last night the shit hit the fan. Dad felt nauseated and they gave him some IV Ativan, which usually works. This time he had an adverse reaction. He was totally sedated but became quite agitated. He pulled out his NG (nasogastric) tube.*
>
> *The night was pretty bad. Plus, I do not like the nurse he had and will not accept her again. She seemed angry with Dad for his behavior and I had to point out to her this morning, when I finally realized it, that it was an adverse reaction and not willful. They tried to re-insert the tube last night but he resisted too much and refused.*
>
> *Today is better. He had to go for an ultrasound of his liver, which turned out to be clear. I think the ultrasound tech was in training because it took over an hour for her to get images, but I have nothing better to do and Dad mostly sleeps.*

They just re-inserted the NG tube. I left the room. He had to agree to it and he did, saying that it would add some humor to his life.

He had the fludarabine last night but they're holding off tonight's dose because his liver enzymes are elevated. He'll probably get it in the morning.

One really nice thing. The resident wart and skin lesion doctor stopped by the other day. She'd been checking on Dad, wondering why he was having so much blood work done, and saw that he was in the hospital. She had wanted to bake him some cookies, but he can't eat, or bring him flowers, but they're not allowed on this unit. So sweet.

I think we're going to be here for a while.

A few days later I wrote to my closest friends and family:

Barry is beginning to feel better physically, but not emotionally. He's in a lot less pain, and also on a lower dose of Dilaudid (opiate). He's way more alert, but very depressed and fatalistic. It's really hard.

And it doesn't help when the attending on rounds talks about "pulling the trigger" on Campath if they think clinically that he's not responding to the nelarabine/fludarabine. All he heard was "pulling the trigger." Terrible metaphor for an oncologist to use.

Also doesn't help when 2 nights ago his oxygen monitor was malfunctioning and beeping loudly quite regularly, or when this unit lost heat overnight.

Nina's been here since Saturday and she leaves tomorrow. All of the kids and the two boys came yesterday for a quick visit. It's been great to have Nina here. She and Michael and the girls will probably come out for Thanksgiving. They're coming at Christmas too. Barry thinks he'll be dead by then.

Hope we'll get out of here sometime. Barry may have to go to an SNF for a while to regain strength and mobility.

As you can tell, I'm exhausted and at the end of my rope. Feeling sorry for myself. Probably not a good time to write.

Hopefully a good night's sleep and continued progress will make tomorrow a better day.

And another one from the next day:

The day started out okay. We both slept much better. Barry even talked about going home. Nina came early, as she was flying home around noon.

Then they rounded. It was appalling. The attending, who has a horrible bedside manner, didn't say anything negative, but his body language and mannerisms were slick and insincere.

Barry only heard his tone, not the content and almost immediately crashed both physically and emotionally. He kept saying "I want to die, I want to die," and asking me to kill him. "My quality of life is non-existent," he said while lying in a hospital bed, hooked up to a million tubes, in pain and drugged (not enjoyably).

Nina talked to the social worker on the unit who promised to get someone, maybe her, to talk to Barry this afternoon, but it never happened. Nina and I were both concerned about leaving him while I drove her to the airport, so Perry rushed over and sat with him while I was gone.

I also emailed David Miklos and he promised to stop by in the afternoon.

The afternoon deteriorated even more. His NG tube (draining his stomach through his nose to prevent nausea and vomiting) dislodged while he was getting up with the OT, and his nurse tried to push it back in. It was torture. I had liked her in the morning, but not anymore. Unfeeling bitch.

The young and completely inexperienced hematology resident came in and started talking hospice and ending treatment. This is what you get in a teaching hospital. Then the palliative care people came in. I really like them but they don't actually know what's going on medically with the cancer. We got a lot more hospice talk.

Finally, David came by about 4:30–5. He is amazing. He told Barry that he isn't dying. He will respect his wishes to stop treatment, but he said that if he went home now he would have to be very heavily medicated and it could take quite a while for him to die. The hematology fellow (I like her) was in the room and asked him what his experience is with PLL patients. David said, "All 3 of them?"

He also said "I'm not your doctor, I'm your friend." What he suggested, and Barry agreed to, was to give the chemo 3–5 more days, maybe do a CT scan and then re-assess. He said he didn't expect a dramatic recovery yet, but more improvement. He also said he would not treat if he didn't think it might work. I told him what I (we) thought of the attending.

Barry lightened up considerably. We talked politics. Barry talked about Torquemada, from the Spanish Inquisition, and recited the Mel Brooks line: "you can't Torquemada anything." Much better.

A really wonderful afternoon nurse re-inserted the NG tube and he's resting peacefully.

Once again I'm hoping for a better day tomorrow."

After sending out that missive, I received a reply from a dear friend who has had her share of cancer and caregiving:

"I am teaching in Manchester today, 80 family therapists who work for the NHS. I am dedicating the day of teaching to the two of you. I am *dedicating it to your sustained ability to articulate your experience honestly and without fear, your ferocity in holding your medical team to the decencies of do no harm and dignity, your allowing us to observe the realities of the vulnerabilities of illness and companionship, and the abiding love you share, even as you see each other in ways one would never wish to. My life is not enriched by knowing about your suffering, but it has more clarity, for which I am profoundly grateful."*

* * *

October 27, 2012
Update on Barry's Health—Slowly Trending Up

Dear Family and Friends,
It's coming up on three weeks since Barry was hospitalized and we're finally starting to see some progress. His cancer, the very rare T-PLL, is in his abdomen and impacting his digestive system. The diagnosis came when they drained the fluid from his abdomen (he had ascites) and tested that. The good news is that it isn't in his marrow and that his graft is intact. He has been treated with two chemos, nelarabine and fludarabine (one course each), and yesterday his symptoms were better enough the docs decided not to move to another treatment, Campath, which comes with a high risk of infection and would most likely impact the graft. So we're glad to avoid it for now.

He's been really sick, lots of abdominal pain and discomfort, and until his digestive system starts working we'll be here. He's on IV nutrition, lots of opiates and has a nasogastric tube in his nose to drain his stomach fluid. The side effects of the chemo are mostly neurological and he's tolerated it well. Since the cancer is not in his marrow, the only way to judge the effectiveness of the treatments is by his symptoms.

I'm staying at the hospital with Barry. There's a fairly comfortable cot here in his room and I'm okay. Having confidence in the medical team here counts for a lot. I'm not nuts about some of the younger residents, but that's the yin and yang of a teaching hospital.

This is all very strange, and once again, the docs are marveling at Barry's weird cancers. David Miklos said that cancer is smart, but we think David is smarter.

Slow, steady progress is what the docs want, and are beginning to see. Let's hope for more.
Much love,
Bonnie

November 3, 2012
Home

Dear Family & Friends,
Things moved quickly and in the right direction since I last wrote to you. On Sunday, Barry's hematologist, Steve Coutre, decided to start Barry on a full course (5 doses) of the second chemo he had been given, fludarabine. Dramatic progress occurred and by Tuesday afternoon, they were able to take the nasogastric tube out. He started eating and drinking (very mild and small amounts) on Wednesday and was released from the hospital yesterday afternoon.
We're very glad to be home after 25 nights in the hospital, although there's a long road ahead. Barry's still very weak. His pain is much reduced and his digestive system is very slowly returning to normal. He will most likely have an abdominal CT scan in a couple of weeks and then another course of fludarabine after Thanksgiving.
Absentee ballots arrived today. We were getting worried. If you're in California: Yes on 30, No on 32, Yes on 34, Yes on 37.
As a good friend said:
Go Giants (done), Go Obama (Tuesday), Go Barry (work in progress).
Love to all,
Bonnie

* * *

BONNIE:

Barry did have another CT and another round of fludarabine right after Thanksgiving. He had pneumonia in December (hospitalization required) and a serious upper respiratory infection in January (no hospitalization required).

February 15, 2013
More Bumps in the Road—Surgery Ahead

Dear Family and Friends,
Next Tuesday (my 65th birthday), Barry will have surgery to hopefully stop the degeneration of his spine. A few weeks ago he started experiencing electrical shocks down his arms and back when he leaned his head forward.
He was referred to a neuro-oncologist who told him that this is Lhermitte's (new vocabulary word) and we needed to find out what was

causing it. We were sent for an emergency MRI because everyone thought it was his leukemia (T-PLL) rearing its ugly head in his spine. Fortunately, no cancer was found, but the neuro-surgeon did further imaging and diagnosed cervical spinal stenosis, most likely caused by the total body irradiation Barry received to prepare him for his second transplant.

The surgery is called posterior surgical decompression and stabilization. The surgeon will take out parts of four vertebrae (C3-C7), put in some bone graft and also titanium rods and screws. The surgery is 3 hours but the recovery will be long, and they warned, painful.

He will be in the hospital for 2–4 days. He will have to wear a hard cervical collar for 8 weeks. After 2 weeks he will get a soft collar for when he's eating and sleeping. Recovery takes anywhere from 3 months to a year. The spinal fusion takes about a year to a year and a half.

There is no other treatment for this condition and it will not improve on its own. Barry's gait is already affected and he cannot pass a sobriety test (heel to toe walking). He has some other neurological deficits as well. The surgeon, Dr. John Ratliff, was concerned that the symptoms came on so quickly.

There are risks to every surgery, and of course, spinal surgery has its own very scary risks. However, Barry is healthy (for him) right now, having survived pneumonia in December and a serious upper respiratory infection in January. The anesthesiologist who we met with yesterday told us that this is a routine surgery and people with Barry's complicated medical history are the norm at Stanford.

Barry's Hematology team has been involved step by step and are totally on board for this surgery.

It wasn't an easy decision to make, but we feel confident that it was the right decision. No guarantees, but the alternative is not pretty.

Please send positive thoughts, prayers, and healing energy our way on Tuesday morning.

Much love,
Bonnie

* * *

BARRY:

Feb 18, 2013:

It is the day before my spinal surgery. I am nervous, fearing the worst—fear itself. We have been getting a barrage of emails from well-wishers and some from folks who've had the operation and survived. I'm told to expect a lot of pain—and a lot of painkillers. Assuming things go as planned, I will be released from the hospital as soon as I can get myself out of bed without help and can take pain meds orally.

Today we film a clip for the Gus Reichbach documentary/memorial. Then it's off to Stanford for some pre-op blood work, a type and screen, and after that, a massage and dinner. Bonnie's sixty-fifth is tomorrow. What a present I'm giving her!

I really don't want to do this, but the tingling in my hands, feet, and back are not going to get better and will probably get worse. I am noticing weakness in my left knee. I am having a lot of trouble playing guitar— missing strings and fumbling chords, so I've put it away. This is a big loss as I'd always imagined playing my guitars right up until my last day. Things just don't fall the way you imagine. I hope I have enough time to recover before cancer throws another punch. Even hurricanes have eyes. I wish I could have a bit of calm so Bonnie and I can do something really nice, like we used to. I don't want to believe that it's all past.

We have our idyllic interlude at the Rosewood in Palo Alto, punctuated by a phone call advising that my operation has been moved up and I need to get to the hospital by five a.m. It will be nearly the last time for two months that I will be able to turn my head. My hands and back tingle, reminding me that I am doing the right thing.

Feb. 19, 2013:

Today is Bonnie's sixty-fifth birthday and the gift I am giving her is an opportunity to hang around a recovery room. I am full of guilt. They put me to sleep and I wake up in the same place. I test fingers and toes. Marvelous, they work! I'm pretty drugged and wearing a hard plastic collar (So I won't bite off my scabs?) but the docs aren't reneging on their prognosis that it will hurt like hell.

It's almost my fastest hospitalization yet. They throw me out Friday afternoon with a cane, a bottle of Flexeril, and a bottle of Vicodin. "See you in a couple of weeks to remove the stitches. Bye!" Yow! It hurts like crazy. Gimme a couple Vicodin for the ride home.

BONNIE:

February 20, 2013
Successful Surgery

Dear Family and Friends,
    Yesterday's surgery went according to plan. We'd been told they were going to send some removed bone to pathology to check for cancer but it looked so good the doctors decided that wasn't necessary.
    Barry's been up a bit today and everyone is marveling at how good he looks and how well he's doing. He's loopy (well loopier than usual) and we're both terribly relieved that this is over. Maybe we can catch a break . . .
    We did celebrate my birthday on Monday night with massages, a lovely dinner and a stay at a beautiful hotel, right before our 4:30 a.m. wakeup call!
    Love,
    Bonnie

* * *

BARRY:

April 7, 2013:

I am quickly recovering from the surgery but not without glitches. After a wonderful visit with my granddaughters, Mimi and Noa, with parents in tow, I develop a respiratory infection, metapneumovirus, to accompany edema (which showed up first in my feet shortly after surgery) and shortness of breath. I'm coughing a lot.

We go to the ITA on April 3 after debating whether we ought to bring the hospital bag. We decide not to; we won't be needing it for this routine visit. They discover I have very low blood pressure and I am hospitalized. Bonnie has to drive all the way back to San Francisco to get it. So much for being an experienced patient and caregiver.

Here I am again—my fifth admission since October. Wes Brown comes to the rescue again. I need prednisone, she says, after the regular attendings are baffled. I'm looking at Monday discharge.

The neck brace provokes coughing and so I remove it. It turns out I don't need it.

May 11, 2013:

On my eight-week post-surgery visit to Dr. Ratliff, he prescribes physical therapy. At my first visit to the therapist, she says I don't need that either. I am strong and have a better range of motion than most people she sees.

But that's far from a clean bill of health. I am now plagued by edema in my legs and gut. I've gained thirty pounds of water weight since the surgery and have submitted to every test in the book to find out why. I've seen Stanford docs who send me back to Dr. Parmer, where it all began. No one has a clue what's causing this water retention and we've tried all the usual treatments, so I'm betting it's those rogue T (for Taliban) cells launching another jihad on my abdomen. I am feeling like the World Trade Center—ground zero for these persistent little guys, but I'm not despondent. Tomorrow is Mother's Day. I am planning to barbeque steaks for my family. The little guys, Silas and Renzo, will be here. It will all be good. That's my goal and enough future for me.

For those readers who are uncertain what edema means, let me just say that the retention of water in between your cells is like pissing into your own body. I bloated up, so that I could not eat. It pressed on my lungs and heart, so I could hardly breathe. Since I couldn't move, my muscles atrophied while the bloat disguised the loss. And who or whatever came up with the torment of edema threw in a giant curve ball—scrotal edema. My scrotum blew up to the size of a summer squash and literally swallowed my penis. I couldn't take a piss until I dug it out, and then there was very iffy aim involved. Bodily functions of all kinds were an ordeal. But to put an objective spin on this narrative, I'll let Bonnie explain:

* * *

BONNIE:

Barry is taken off of acyclovir and develops shingles. He is hospitalized once again but fortunately the pain is less than he fears and he gets treatments that work. Unfortunately, this hospitalization is from late June to early July, the worst time to be in a teaching hospital. Everything takes forever and there are too many newbies around. He is still on Hematology Service and, quite frankly, no one seems to be in charge. His edema is getting worse. He is referred to cardiology and then to an edema specialist (another new specialty we've never heard of). Cardiology doesn't think it's his heart and the edema specialist, the best in the country, comes up with an idea that really doesn't float and treatments that do nothing as well. We consult regularly with David Miklos and Wes Brown but they're not in charge either. Docs have ruled out heart, kidney (kidney doc says his kidneys are innocent bystanders) and cancer (always looking for cancer). We begin to feel desperate but are able to go on a wonderful spa vacation in early June.

August 8, 2013
Enough with the Hospital Already

Dear Family and Friends,
Yesterday we returned home after yet another hospitalization, Barry's 12th. This one was for 16 nights. It's been a terrible year, one thing after another. There's been cancer relapse, many upper respiratory infections (some requiring hospitalization), a reactivation of Barry's shingles, spinal surgery, and now—since March—edema that won't quit or respond to any treatment.

Barry put on 40 lbs. of fluid weight and was having extreme difficulty moving and eating; finally, what brought us to the hospital was extreme shortness of breath. After many exhaustive tests, all of the really bad things were ruled out—heart, kidney, liver, and of course, cancer.

The diagnosis now is chronic graft vs. host disease (cGVHD), with an unusual presentation. What else is new? Barry has always had unusual presentations, weird symptoms, and also extremely rare conditions and diagnoses. Every new doctor, and we saw many at Stanford during this stay, is amazed after reading Barry's medical record. But he's still standing, eight years after the first cancer diagnosis.

Graft vs. host disease is a complication that can occur after a stem cell or bone marrow transplant in which the newly transplanted donor cells attack the transplant recipient's body. So Barry is under attack, but thankfully cGVHD is treatable and it also means he's got a graft. He's on steroids now and we will find out soon if other immunosuppressants might be used. His edema is much better, but he is very, very weak.

We're very happy to be home and very grateful to the BMT (Blood and Marrow Transplant) team at Stanford, especially David Miklos and Wes Brown. They're the ones who came up with the cGVHD diagnosis and who understand Barry so well. He's obviously got a ton of underlying strength and health (weirdly) to bounce back after all of this, including of course, two transplants. One nurse compared him to a cat.

We don't want to go back to Stanford Hospital, our home away from

*home. I am way too familiar with the layout, the senior discount in the
cafeteria, the cots, the parking workarounds, and the rules and how to
flaunt them. Hopefully we will not return until the new hospital has been
built (2017) and beyond, but that's probably a bit of wishful thinking.*

Much love to all,

Bonnie

Barry is hospitalized two more times, only a few days apart each time. After one hospitalization he recovers for a few days at the rehab unit of the Jewish Home in San Francisco, very close to our house. He is very weakened and cannot make it up our stairs. He is becoming a prisoner in our home of 41 years. We begin to look for a more manageable home.

Many not so wonderful things happen during these hospitalizations, none of which are, thankfully, life threatening, but some cause needless horrible symptoms and necessitate more hospitalizations.

Stanford is a teaching hospital, and I was forced to do some teaching when I gave some "feedback" to an attending physician. During these hospitalizations Barry had a right heart catheterization, PET-CT, endoscopy and many other tests that essentially ruled out anything other than chronic graft vs. host disease. The last hospitalization came as a result of an episode at the ITA where Barry experienced severe vomiting, chest pain, and almost passed out. Stroke and heart attack were ruled out, but after an endoscopy we were told that he was one step away from "hamburger esophagus" as a result of NG tubes and other assaults on his body. It sounds like a dinner dish, but I assure you, it's not. His throat was beginning to look like hamburger meat.

Aug 31, 2013

More News—All Good

Dear Family and Friends,

When I last wrote we had just returned from yet another long hospitalization. There were two shorter ones that followed very closely, but Barry is finally on the mend. I will spare you the details, but suffice it to say that he has had every test known to medicine, some more than once, and except for the chronic graft vs. host disease (cGVHD), has been given a clean bill of health for now. He is very weak but is eating well, after months of not being able to. He is getting stronger and we are both optimistic about the future. For those of you who know Barry well, optimism is not usually in his vocabulary.

On the way home from the hospital this last time we bought a house! As many of you know, we have two flights up to the front door and many interior stairs that, as we age, make it difficult to live here. We've been in this house for almost 41 years and it has served us well. We've been looking for many months for a more manageable abode, and last week a house that was beyond our price range was reduced so we jumped on it. I had an appointment to see it on Friday while Barry was still in the hospital. Fortunately, and surprisingly, he got released in time to see it. We put in an offer that afternoon and it was accepted a few hours later. It's got 99% of what we want/need, including wonderful grandchildren space, and we will be moving sometime near the end of September. I have hired people to help me sort through, get rid of, and pack up our house—a daunting prospect after 41 years. We will have it staged and put on the market after we leave. We will miss Glen Park a lot, as well as (most of) our neighbors and friends in the hood. We will not miss the stairs.

Much love to everyone and a sweet, healthy, and happy New Year to all,

Bonnie

* * *

BARRY:

I was attentive to the karma. On Friday morning the doctors made their rounds. At the end, I hesitantly broached the question: "When can I expect to get discharged?" They said I could leave that morning, if I wanted to, and I did. I got to see the house and participate in the purchase. I could hardly conceal my joy at doing something "real world" and exciting.

I am thin as a rail. I weigh what I did in the eighth grade, having lost most of my muscle mass, but I have home PT and am strictly following the regimen. I am still weak but getting stronger by the day and feeling a restoration of energy. Drs. Brown and Miklos are looking after my medical needs. Bonnie continues to work night and day to keep me on track, but I am doing more and more, so I hope I am lightening her load. We are both looking forward to moving into a house with better access, although I am not quite as housebound as I was and, if I dare to prognosticate, I think I am going to get a lot better. While I may be required to take meds for quite a while to keep cGVHD at bay, at least they are working for me.

SO WE BEGIN a new year (5774 by the Hebrew calendar) with a sense of optimism and hope. To me, there's no mistaking the karma.

Barry's Epilogue

On Sept. 20, 2013, Dr. David Miklos wrote:

Hi Barry and Bonnie,
I have exciting news.
Using your ascites from October 2012, Sequenta identified your T cell PLL cancer sequence (It's both TCG and TCB).
Running your Blood sample for a quantitative T cell high throughput sequencing MRD, you had 16.37 cancer clones in a million WBC.
That's 0.000016% PLL.
Your cancer is less than 1/10,000 and thus MRD negative by current criteria. Your CLL has been undetectable.
Perhaps more importantly, we can accurately and sensitively quantify both of your cancers going forward. No more mystery about whether the cancer is in the ascites or any tissue for that matter.
So, we will manage your cGVHD and hope for the best with MORE confidence.
We hope you guys are loving your new DIGS
Congrats again!
I told you we'd get this to work
Enjoy your new home and see you 10/4!
David

For those of you who fade out when you attempt to read "medispeak," what he is saying is that he can find no evidence of CLL and my T-PLL shows about 16 clonal cells out of a million. When I was first diagnosed with CLL, they saw a clonal population of T cells but the diagnostic tools they used eight years ago were blunt instruments compared to what they just did. David collaborated on a new-fangled test that goes where no cancer researcher has gone before and is now able to look at miniscule samples of blood. He is a relentless pursuer of cancer evidence and will not cease his searching until he finds some. I'd have preferred he stopped in the ten thousand-cell range so I'd have an "undetectable" verdict, but no, David has to go to the millions. Lo and behold he found a few. (I couldn't let him go away hungry.) Still, I'm okay with miniscule. I bet most of us have that kind of cell floating around inside. So, for now, I'm well—a bit weak from the last year's travails, but well none-the-less. It's way better than being asymptomatic.

Dec. 27, 2013:

Where do you end a story like this? It's like making the horizon your destination. Throughout, I've said, even if you're so-called "cured" there's always another test scheduled and always reason to worry. The prednisone has done what we expected it to do, including bestowing on my bod its cornucopia of side effects. I have lost two inches in height that I'll never get back. They say it's prednisone-induced osteoporosis. I've also been diagnosed with diabetes. Again prednisone is the culprit. This they might be able to reverse. I have plenty of slow-healing bruises on my hands and arms. I have been prescribed a statin, though Medicare and my doc don't see eye-to-eye on the right one. But I've got no ascites. No edema. My pharmacological regimen is at once impressive and depressing. Plus, I HATE eating healthy, as required of diabetics who wish to improve their condition. I worked out today and feel none the worse for wear. My two granddaughters, Mimi and Noa, are in town and I find myself smiling all the time. So, I'd be a shmuck to kvetch.

Bonnie's Epilogue

Barry was hospitalized on January 16 with similar symptoms to his relapse in the Fall of 2012 and his GVHD in the summer or 2013. This turned out to be his final relapse. David Miklos was there for us in every way and we finally had "the conversation." Barry was sent home with hospice. He died 27 hours later.

January 29, 2014
Home with Hospice

Dear Family and Friends,
  Barry's been in the hospital for almost two weeks with another relapse of his T-PLL. He's been in intense abdominal pain. He had a round of chemo (fludarabine) but it has not worked. We are going home tomorrow and hospice has been called in.
  The cancer is winning. It's difficult to accept, but when the suffering is so intense, it is easier.
  The hematology attending doc cried with me as she told me how hard it had been to see his suffering.
  He's resting peacefully now. All treatment has ended and he is going home with only IV pain meds and an abdominal drain. We will all work together to make him comfortable and hope for a peaceful passing.
  Love to all,
  Bonnie, Megan, Nina, and Julia

* * *

BONNIE:

So after eight and a half years, sixteen hospitalizations, seventeen bone marrow biopsies and more infections than are fathomable, Barry passed on. He died peacefully at home surrounded by his family.

A day after he died, David Miklos wrote this email to the BMT Team at Stanford

Barry Willdorf died peacefully at home surrounded by his family Bonnie, Megan, Nina, and Julia early Saturday morning.

I first met Barry July 2006 when he sought care for his chronic lymphocytic leukemia (CLL).

Barry was originally my transplant patient, always my friend, and now my immortal inspiration.

I am passing along funeral plans for Barry.

The funeral will be at 10 am on Tuesday at Beth Israel Judea on Brotherhood Way.

Bonnie will be sitting shiva on Tuesday, Wednesday, and Thursday at their house at 116 De Soto Street from 4 pm with services at 6 pm.

His obituary, which will be published tomorrow, is at http://www.legacy.com/obituaries/sfgate/obituary.aspx?page= lifestory&pid=169439094.

In 2008 Barry wrote an autobiographical piece for the 40th Reunion of the Columbia Strike http://www.columbia1968.com/barry-willdorf/.

Please take a moment to visit his web page: http://agauchepress.com

Finally, I'm pasting his blog posting when he first thanked Stanford BMT.

It can be retrieved from google typing "Willdorf, Miklos, 10 commandments."

We miss you Barry. On behalf of Barry and Bonnie—Thank you Stanford BMT and Heme.

David

Afterword

There were many things we both learned during the eight and a half years between Barry's diagnosis and his death.

- Doctors and nurses are not our priority. The patient is the priority. It is really important to speak up if you think something is wrong, either with someone's treatment of you, like a nurse being rude, unfeeling, or incompetent, a doctor who is miscommunicating, or in over his or her head, or any medical professional overstepping his or her bounds. These all happened to us and we both felt good about any changes we made happen or any complaints that we made that were heard. Don't be afraid to speak up.
- We all want doctors to know everything, and to be able to fix it. This is never going to happen. They do their best, and that's all we can hope for.
- Not everyone in your family or community is going to be helpful. We were very lucky that our family was so supportive and loving. There were a (really very) few friends who either disappeared, or were so unhelpful that we just severed contact. We found that we did not really want people's advice, just love and support.

A mantra that I learned and try to live by:

JUST THIS
DON'T KNOW
PRESENT MOMENT
ONLY MOMENT

March 2013. Barry, Bonnie, and grandchildren

March 2014. Willdorfs and Donor Family

Appendix

BARRY'S OBITUARY

Barry passed away peacefully at his home on February 1, 2014, surrounded by his family. The cause was leukemia. He had been treated for 8.5 years at Stanford, where he had received two stem cell transplants. He is survived by his wife, Bonnie of 45 years, three daughters, Megan Willdorf, Nina (Michael) Endelman, and Julia (Nick) Campins, and four grandchildren.

A life-long activist, Barry was born in New York on March 6, 1945. He grew up in Malden and in Gloucester, Massachusetts. Barry attended Colby College in Maine and the University of Manchester, in Manchester, England, where he studied history and economics. He attended Columbia Law School in New York, where he was an active member of Students for a Democratic Society (SDS), an anti-war organization. He and Bonnie Offner were married June 1968. After graduation from Columbia in 1969, he practiced law with the Legal Aid Society in New York City. He and Bonnie moved to Southern California in 1970, where he founded, near the height of the Vietnam War, the Southern California Military Law Project, an organization that defended servicemen charged with violations of military law. His semi-autobiographical novel, *Bring the War Home!*, is based on this period in their lives. Barry also co-authored a self-help book for military personnel. In 1971, he and Bonnie moved to San Francisco. Barry opened his law practice in San Francisco, practicing criminal, and eventually civil law. For many years, he practiced with his longtime legal partner, Laura Stevens. Over the course of several decades, he litigated hundreds of cases, representing employees, actors, artists, victims of investment and real estate fraud, and tenants.

In 2005, the San Francisco AIDS Legal Referral Panel named him

Lawyer of the Year for groundbreaking work on behalf of AIDS patients, including the case of Daniels v. CVS. Barry often made headlines for the controversial cases he handled, including the wrongful death of a woman on welfare and the swindle of investors in a South African gold mine. In his last case, he and Laura won a multimillion dollar jury verdict against a Bay Area landlord who regularly cheated his tenants out of their security deposits. As his legal career wound down and as he became a grandfather, he turned increasingly to writing and published five novels. Those who knew him remember him as a loyal friend, loving husband, father, and grandfather, a warm host, and a fierce advocate, ready to take a case, defend the defenseless and comfort the afflicted.

Funeral services at Beth Isreal Judea, 625 Brotherhood Way, San Francisco on Tuesday at 10:00 a.m. In lieu of flowers, please send donations to the Hope Reichbach Fund, hopeforbrooklyn.com.

MEGAN'S EULOGY

As I sat down to write this, it felt so surreal. I tried to prepare myself for this moment and now that it's here, it all feels so foreign. Reflecting on positive memories, so many flood back. Forty years of memories with both of my parents present every step of the way. I now see how rare that is. I am beyond lucky to have had a dad who had such a profound depth of love.

He gave us all a rich life filled with adventure, travel, and exposure to arts and culture. He instilled in me the strength to hold different opinions and to stand up for what I believed. When I came home with endless report cards saying that I was a good student, but that I needed to stop talking so much in class and be less critical of others' comments, he would say, "That's my girl. It proves you have a strong personality and you're intelligent." Freshman year in high school, when I got caught by the BART police for using a child's pass, they called home to tell my parents. My father said he'd give me a strict talking to when I got home. The minute I walked in the door, he gave me one of those Barry smirk/grins and high-fived me for bucking the system.

He was proud of me when I wasn't proud of myself. He was hard on me at times. I made poor decisions and at those times I felt resentment and judgment. Nine out of ten times he was right. Ten out of ten times it was from a place of love and protection.

When I worked with him on his last big case, a class-action lawsuit, I felt he gained a whole new respect for me, and we became so much closer. I'm so thankful for that.

But one of the things I'm most thankful for is that one month ago at my 40th birthday dinner, my whole family was together for the last time. He got to see all of his children and grandchildren, got to watch all 4 of the little ones sitting at their tiny table drawing together and periodically giving him big hugs. He got to celebrate a happy occasion in a brief moment that he felt well enough to get out of the house. That night, my dad read the most beautiful speech. I feel like it's everything he ever wanted to say to me and I felt more loved than ever. I take pleasure in knowing that, between us, nothing was left unsaid. Dad I will miss you deeply. I will talk to you often and I will love you forever.

NINA'S EULOGY

You might think that given how epic my dad's struggle with leukemia has been, we would have had ample time to plan what to say at his funeral.

And yet, I feel unprepared for this moment. I think that speaks to his incredible resilience and strength. His passing was an impossibility. He would always find a way to pull through. He was an ox. And he was supported by my mother, the most relentless, resourceful, and loving partner and friend you could ever imagine.

My father was a force to be reckoned with, a fighter for better or for worse. At times, I found him to be a bit of an ideologue, but that's just because no one had more courage of his own convictions. The pride he showed in helping people, in righting wrongs was something we could all learn from. He taught me and my sisters that the best thing we could do with our lives was to make a difference in other people's lives. Honestly, he couldn't care less WHAT we did as long as we did something that mattered.

My father was quiet about his achievements. He was unshowy and actually kind of insular in his own way. Once you got him talking, you would learn so much. He taught me one of the most important lessons I ever learned about writing. Never fall in love with a single word. In high school, he was reading over something I wrote and I was stumbling over the beginning of an essay. He explained that while you really might love a word, sometimes it'll just clunk up your thinking in your effort to make it work. Throw it out. Let it go. I still think about that so often in my work.

Over the past several years, with the arrival of grandchildren, we all saw my dad soften. As kids, we used to call him an ogre (he had a big bark), but the ogre turned into a softie. He took immense pleasure in tasks like brushing my daughter Mimi's hair after a bath. That was his job, and boy did he enjoy it.

He also started to become more chatty, more leisurely in his curiosity. When I'd call the house, and my mother was out, he would say, "Bonnie's out, you can call back in a couple hours." And then we'd get to talking ourselves. He was full of questions, thoughts, anecdotes. He would soak up every little detail of his granddaughters' lives, kvelling in his own way.

Over the holidays, we were sitting on the back deck of their new house and he was excited to tell me that he and my mom were just about done with their draft of the new book they were writing about navigating cancer together. The challenge, he was explaining, was figuring out how to end the book. How do you end a book about cancer when it is a constant?

The working title of the book is *Dancing with Cancer*. I told him I thought that was a weird title. I pressed him pretty hard. He explained he didn't like to think about his relationship with cancer like a fight, which is the way people commonly talk about the disease: it's a battle, you struggle with it. Someone wins, someone loses.

And yet, in my mind, to say that you're dancing seemed a little too diplomatic and elegant for how gruesome and difficult the past several years had been for him.

In my father's final hours, my mother and sisters and I sat with him at home, talking, reminiscing, laughing, crying. He was peaceful and calm, and we feel he was soaking up our love. It was clear that his dancing metaphor was an apt one; it wasn't a fight at that point. And ultimately the final move in the dance was his—a beautiful, graceful bow.

JULIA'S EULOGY

I sometimes thought my dad was the most interesting man in the world. He is the reason that I grew up thinking that once you become a father, you suddenly know everything.

He had such killer stories. He surfed in a hurricane, fell into a cesspool during a hurricane (do you sense a theme?). He got kicked out of the draft, yet was more knowledgeable about the military than anyone I know.

He was the only person I knew who had (at least claimed to) broken every finger on both hands, as well as his ear. He built a house. Not because he knew how, but he had always wanted to. So he figured out how to, and he did it.

And he didn't just toe the party line or think what he was taught to think. Whenever dad thought about something, he thought about it deeply and came up with a nuanced view. He was a lefty liberal who owned guns but believed in gun control. Knee-jerk wasn't a word you could ever tag him with, although I'm sure at various times, "jerk" was. And that was part of why we all loved him—he didn't take bullshit. (I am not going to talk about him as a grandfather, because I'd like to give myself a chance to make it through.)

I remember when I was a kid, I was pretty sure I knew what lawyers did. They sat in a chair with their feet on a windowsill and talked on speakerphone. Given how much my dad and I both hate the phone, it seems like a perfect job for both of us, no? I also knew it meant that every so often, when you go to trial, you come home with a bunch of binders. I'm lucky enough to have some of those binders in my office now, along with a stapler with a label that says "DO NOT TAKE THIS AWAY FROM HERE!!!!!" (with five exclamation points).

He was so supportive of my career, even though he had always told me not to become a lawyer. I knew I could open my own firm because I saw him do it. He didn't just give me binders and a stapler. When I opened my firm, we sat down and he gave me a list of people to tell and ways to market it. He gave me confidence and useful advice.

After having connected as a father and tom-boy daughter over sports, as an adult over politics and law, and as a parent over my kids, he gave me one last gift, as a fellow entrepreneurial lawyer.

So, these are the things my dad taught me:

- Hockey is a beautiful game.
- There is only so much fat in the world. If one person loses weight, another person has to gain weight.
- The reason it always feels like the walk back from your destination is shorter than the walk to it is that when you were walking there, you were walking against the rotation of the earth, and on the way back,

you were walking with the rotation of the earth.

- If you are going to have an opinion, have an opinion worth having. Listen to people, but stick to your guns.
- You can be a trial lawyer and be home for dinner every night.
- You can have conflicts with your family, but if someone from the outside slights them, you are the first line of defense and their fiercest defender. Always stand behind your spouse.
- You have two kinds of family, the family you're born with and the family you choose. I'm lucky that, unlike my dad, I have good relationships with the family I was born with, but I also treasure deeply the family he and my mom chose, and do the same with the family I have chosen.

Acknowledgments

Many people helped along the way. I want to especially thank my writer/reader friends, Kaethe Weingarten, Mary Winegarden, and Roslyn Banish for their invaluable comments and support. I also want to thank Jean Vengua for her close and clear editing and Hilton Obenzinger for his coaching and help with the publishing process.

Books by Barry S. Willdorf   *Photo by Roslyn Banish*

About the Authors

BARRY S. WILLDORF

Barry grew up in Malden and Gloucester, MA, where he was the first person to surf the North Shore of Massachusetts. He graduated from Colby College in 1966 with a B.A. in History and earned a J.D. from Columbia Law School in 1969. He also attended the University of Manchester in England in the mid-sixties.

In 1970, Barry founded the Southern California Military Law Project, one of a handful of legal defense organizations dedicated to providing military personal with civilian defense counsel. He continued representing members of the armed forces until 1975. During that time, he co-authored a legal self-help book for military personnel: *Turning the Regs Around.* In 2001, Barry published a semi-autobiographical novel, *Bring the War Home!* fictionalizing his experiences representing anti-war Marines at Camp Pendleton, CA in 1970 and 1971.

During a legal career spanning four decades, he defended clients charged with serious felonies and represented hundreds of victims of securities and real estate fraud. He served as a Judge Pro Tem in the San Francisco Superior Courts and was a member of the panels of arbitrators for NASD, NYSE and Kaiser Permanente.

His legal publishing credits include co-authoring *How To Pass the LSATs*, Monarch Press, 1969, a chapter in Matthew Bender, *California Forms of Jury Instructions*, relating to real estate brokers, appraisers, and notaries. He was a contributing editor for Matthew Bender's *Trial Master* series. His op-ed, "A Cloud On Impartiality: Has Clarence Thomas Committed Impeachable of Prosecutable Offenses?" was published by the *Daily Journal* (a San Francisco and Los Angeles law journal) in November 2011. He also published several op-ed pieces on the Second Amendment.

Barry was also the author of four novels. His historical novel, *The Flight of the Sorceress*, (Wild Child Publishing, 2010) won a Global E-Book Award and was a finalist for an EPIC award. His "1970s Trilogy", *Burning Questions, A Shot In The Arm,* and *The Fourth Conspirator,* published by Whiskey Creek Press have received many five-star reviews.

BONNIE WILLDORF

Bonnie is a graduate of Barnard College and the University of California, Berkeley, where she received a Masters in Library Science. She was a long-time Director of the Resource Center for Alumnae Resources, a groundbreaking women's career development non-profit. After stints managing content for two high-tech start-ups, Bonnie became the regional librarian for the West Coast offices of a major engineering firm and was a officer in the local chapter of the Special Libraries Association. Her publications include *The Liberal Arts Job Search in an Electronic Environment: The Founding and Development of Alumnae Resources,* Haworth Press, 1996.

She lives in San Francisco surrounded by her three grown daughters, four grandchildren and many friends.

66728686R00129

Made in the USA
Charleston, SC
29 January 2017